SUPER CROCS & MONSTER WINGS

super crocs &
MONSter WiNGS

MODERN ANIMALS' ANCIENT PAST

CLaire EaMer

annick press
toronto + new york + vancouver

Annick Press Ltd.

Edited by Elizabeth McLean
Photo research by Claire Eamer
Cover and interior design by Lisa Hemingway
Cover illustration *(Sarcosuchus imperator)* by John Sibbick
Cover photo (Nile crocodile) by EcoPrint/shutterstock.com

We acknowledge the support of the Canada Council for the Arts, the Ontario Arts Council, the Government of Canada through the Book Publishing Industry Development Program (BPIDP), and the Ontario Book Publishing Tax Credit (OBPTC) for our publishing activities.

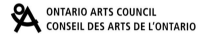

ONTARIO ARTS COUNCIL
CONSEIL DES ARTS DE L'ONTARIO

Cataloguing in Publication

Eamer, Claire, 1947–
    Super crocs and monster wings : modern animals' ancient past / by Claire Eamer.

Includes bibliographical references and index.
ISBN 978-1-55451-130-3 (bound)
ISBN 978-1-55451-129-7 (pbk.)
    1. Evolution (Biology)—Juvenile literature. 2. Phylogeny—Juvenile literature.
    3. Animals—Juvenile literature. I. Title.

QH367.1.E24 2008   j591.3'8   C2007-905212-6

Printed and bound in China.

Published in the U.S.A. by	**Distributed in Canada by**	**Distributed in the U.S.A. by**
Annick Press (U.S.) Ltd.	Firefly Books Ltd.	Firefly Books (U.S.) Inc.
	66 Leek Crescent	P.O. Box 1338
	Richmond Hill, ON	Ellicott Station
	L4B 1H1	Buffalo, NY 14205

Visit our website at: **www.annickpress.com**.

CONTENTS

STRANGE RELATIVES

Many scientists think birds may be descended from dinosaurs like this therapod.

WHEN YOU GO FOR a walk in a park, what animals do you see? Maybe a sparrow pecking at seeds, a squirrel chattering from a branch, a woodpecker rat-a-tat-tatting on a tree, or ants bustling over the path.

The world is full of animals, amazing animals. But they're only a tiny fraction of the animals that have lived on Earth over the past hundreds of millions of years.

About 99 percent of all the species that ever lived are already extinct, gone forever. Some died in huge global catastrophes. Some gradually disappeared as the world around them changed. Some were transformed beyond recognition by evolution.

However, many haven't disappeared entirely. They have relatives living today—direct descendants, or distant cousins, or other branches of huge and ancient families.

6

Remember the sparrow in the park? Imagine it surrounded by the spirits of all its extinct relations. There would be small, feathered birds; large birdlike creatures with claws on their wings; dinosaurs with powerful hind legs and mouths full of sharp teeth; faint, ancient ghosts of four-legged reptiles the size of dogs. And behind them, in the shadows, even more distant and alien life forms. All are part of the evolutionary path that led to that sparrow.

This book is about strange relatives—ancient animals and their living relations. Some of the ancient animals are so odd and unexpected that you'll look at their modern relatives in a new way.

Some of the modern animals are odd and unexpected too!

A white-crowned sparrow looks up from its seed dinner.

A toolkit of words

SCIENCE HAS DEVELOPED handy tools for talking about the history of life on Earth. In fact, it's hard to talk about the ancient past and ancient animals without using them.

One tool is the geologic time scale. Another is the system of scientific names for all plants and animals. Here's how they work.

WORDS FOR TIME

THE EARTH HAS BEEN around for about 4.5 billion years. That's so long, it's hard even to think about it. If the whole 4.5 billion years were laid out on a clock face, the 65 million years since dinosaurs went extinct would fit into the last 10 minutes of the last hour.

To make it easier to talk about such huge stretches of time, scientists use a time scale based on fossils and rock layers. The table below shows the major divisions of geologic time, and some of the smaller divisions that are important to our story.

EON	ERA	PERIOD		EPOCH	YEARS AGO
Phanerozoic 543 MYA* to today	**Cenozoic** 65 MYA* to today	**Quaternary** 2.6 MYA* to today		**Holocene**	10,000 years ago to today
				Pleistocene	2.6 MYA* to 10,000 years ago
		Tertiary	**Neogene** 23.8 to 2.6 MYA	**Pliocene**	5.3 to 2.6 MYA
				Miocene	23.8 to 5.3 MYA
			Paleogene 65 to 23.8 MYA	**Oligocene**	33.7 to 23.8 MYA
				Eocene	54.8 to 33.7 MYA
				Paleocene	65 to 54.8 MYA
	Mesozoic 248 to 65 MYA	**Cretaceous**			144 to 65 MYA
		Jurassic			206 to 144 MYA
		Triassic			248 to 206 MYA
	Paleozoic 543 to 248 MYA	**Permian**			290 to 248 MYA
		Carboniferous			354 to 290 MYA
		Devonian			417 to 354 MYA
		Silurian			443 to 417 MYA
		Ordovician			490 to 443 MYA
		Cambrian			543 to 490 MYA
Precambrian 4500 to 543 MYA	**Proterozoic**				2500 to 543 MYA
	Archean				3800 to 2500 MYA
	Hadean				4500 to 3800 MYA

*MYA = million years ago

WORDS FOR ANIMALS

ALL ANIMALS, EXTINCT or living, have scientific names. In the case of prehistoric animals, the scientific name is often the only name they have—like *Tyrannosaurus rex*, the most famous of all dinosaurs.

The naming system was developed about 300 years ago by a Swedish naturalist called Linnaeus. He decided to classify and name all plants and animals in a way that explained their relationship to each other.

For example, here's how the system describes a lion:

KINGDOM: Animalia (all animals)

PHYLUM: Chordata (animals with backbones, commonly called chordates)

CLASS: Mammalia (mammals, or warm-blooded chordates that have hair and suckle their young)

ORDER: Carnivora (all mammals that are meat-eaters)

FAMILY: Felidae (all cats, large and small)

GENUS: *Panthera* (large cats with a special larynx that lets them roar as well as purr)

SPECIES: *leo* (the lion)

The lion's scientific name is made up of the genus name and the species name: *Panthera leo*. It's traditional to print both parts of the name underlined or in italics.

The African lion's scientific name, *Panthera leo*, comes from the Latin word for lion, *leo*, which also gives us names like Leonard and Leona.

9

THE CHANGING SHAPE OF THE EARTH

Nothing remains the same forever on our planet—not even the ground beneath our feet.

Earth's outer crust is made of huge plates that float slowly on the molten inner core, forming the continents and ocean bottoms. Sometimes the plates collide and sometimes they pull apart. The process is called plate tectonics. Over billions of years, this process has shifted continents around, and even opened and closed oceans.

▶ About 340 million years ago, most of the world's land was moving together to form a single big continent called Pangaea (pan-JEE-ah).

▶ By 250 million years ago, North America and Eurasia had drifted north of the equator, but South America, Africa, Australia, Antarctica, and India were still joined in one big land mass called Gondwana.

▶ At 150 million years ago, the Atlantic Ocean had begun to push North America and Europe apart. A narrow body of water also separated Antarctica and Australia from the joined continents of South America and Africa, and India had just begun to migrate northward.

10

Earth, 340 million years ago: The southern continent, Gondwana, is moving northward and will soon collide with the center continent, made up of North America and northern Europe. They will form one huge continent, called Pangaea. The land mass at the top of the map will later become Siberia.

▶ About 50 million years ago, Australia had broken free from Antarctica and was heading north. South America and Africa had moved apart, but North America and South America were still separated by ocean.

▶ By 5 million years ago, a string of islands linked North America and South America. Within a couple of million years more, an unbroken strip of land joined the two continents.

Earth is still changing, even as I write this and you read it. The Atlantic Ocean is getting wider about half as quickly as your fingernails grow. Volcanoes are building new islands in the Pacific Ocean. In northern Canada, land that was squashed down by glaciers in the last ice age is bouncing back up.

In the future, the planet will be a very different place—just as it was in the past.

11

The Changing Shape of the Earth

MONSTERS ²
WITH GOSSAMER WINGS

Meganeura soars in its ancient world, thanks to an artist's carefully researched painting.

IN SUMMER, DRAGONFLIES skim low over lakes and ponds. Their twig-like bodies and fragile wings glitter in sunlight. They're flashy and beautiful, but not scary unless you're the size of a mosquito.

Once upon a time, however, dragonflies were monsters, the largest flying creatures alive—and very scary indeed.

RULER OF THE ANCIENT SKIES

ON A SPRING DAY 325 million years ago, a fat fly the size of a chickadee settled on a bristly swamp plant called a horsetail. A shower had just passed, and water dripped from huge tree-like mosses and ferns in the surrounding

12

Super Crocs & Monster Wings

forest. The fly stretched its wings in the sun's warmth, trusting the plant to hide it from danger.

But danger found it. A swish of air, four huge transparent wings veined like church windows, a flash of metallic color—and *Meganeura* had its dinner!

Meganeura monyi was a giant dragonfly, more than five times the size of the largest dragonfly alive today. *Meganeura* ruled Earth's skies during the Carboniferous period, 100 million years before the time of dinosaurs.

THE SHAPE OF MEGANEURA'S WORLD

MEGANEURA MONYI'S FOSSIL remains were found in France. Fossils of related giant dragonflies from the same period have turned up in Australia, North America, Russia, and in the roof of an English coal mine. In *Meganeura*'s day, all of those places were part of the one big continent of Pangaea. Near the equator Pangaea was warm and much of it was covered with fern forests and lush swamps. That's where *Meganeura* lived and died.

Eventually, the forests and swamps died too. Over time, they were buried, compressed, and transformed into carbon in the form of coal. Beneath the surface of Britain, northern Europe, Asia, and large parts of North America lie huge deposits of coal from those ancient swamps. That's why the time when the swamps thrived is called the Carboniferous period and why *Meganeura*'s home is often referred to as "the coal swamps."

With plenty of prey in the coal swamps, *Meganeura* feasted and grew big—really big. Its wingspread, tip to tip, was almost as wide as your bedroom door, and its body was as thick as the handlebar of a bicycle.

13

The stiff veins show black against the transparent membrane of the wings on this cherry-faced meadowhawk.

WINGS tell a tale

DESPITE ITS SIZE, MEGANEURA was definitely a dragonfly. The proof is in the wings.

A dragonfly has two long, skinny wings on each side of its body. The wings are thin sheets of tissue supported by a network of veins. That's what you see in fossil imprints of *Meganeura* wings.

When a dragonfly first becomes an adult, its wings are soft and flexible. It pumps fluid into the wing veins to make them strong and stiff, just as air pumped into a bicycle tire makes it round and hard. *Meganeura*'s wings had a special design feature that gave them extra strength. Half the veins that ran the length of the wings were located on the wing's top and half on the bottom. These alternating veins created a rigid structure like corrugated cardboard.

Once the dragonfly's wings have stiffened, it can fly. And can it ever fly!

Dragonflies are the acrobats of the air. Their wings swivel, tilt, work in pairs or all together, flap in the same direction, or flap in opposite directions. Modern dragonflies can glide, fly forward, fly backward, or spin on the spot. They can hover in one place or zip along almost as fast as a car on the highway.

Could *Meganeura* do the same thing?

Because it was so big, *Meganeura* had to push a lot of air around with its wings in order to fly. Pushing air is such hard work that scientists once thought the best *Meganeura* could manage was a clumsy glide through the air.

A couple of recent discoveries have changed their minds.

14

German model-maker Susanne Leidenroth shows off her replica of *Meganeuropsis*, a giant dragonfly that lived several million years after *Meganeura*.

FUN FacTS

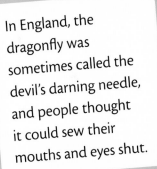

A scanning electron microscope reveals tiny individual eyes that make up a dragonfly's compound eyes. The hairs probably sense air speed during flight.

Meganeuropsis permiana, a giant dragonfly that lived a little later than *Meganeura,* is the only one to challenge *Meganeura* in the size stakes. Fossils found so far show it was at least as big, and maybe even bigger.

Dragonflies have two huge compound eyes, each one made up of 30,000 smaller eyes. They clean them with special brushes built into their front legs.

Dragonfly nymphs are jet-propelled. They breathe through gills located in their rectums. The nymph sucks water in through its anus, extracts the oxygen with its gills, and squirts the water back out, producing a jet-engine effect that shoots the nymph through the water.

In England, the dragonfly was sometimes called the devil's darning needle, and people thought it could sew their mouths and eyes shut.

Today's dragonflies are midgets compared to *Meganeura* and the other ancient giants. *Petalura gigantea,* a rare dragonfly from southeastern Australia, is one of the largest. Its body can be longer than a man's finger, and its wingspan is about the length of a ballpoint pen.

An average-sized modern dragonfly can eat 300 mosquitoes a day. Imagine what *Meganeura* could eat!

THe MYStery OF MeGaNeura FLiGHt

THE FIRST DISCOVERY WAS fossils showing details of the giant dragon-fly's wing structure. Scientists studying the fossils say the wings clearly would have worked. *Meganeura* was indeed an active flier.

But wing structure isn't enough. Flying takes a lot of muscle power, and muscles need oxygen to work. Until recently, no one thought the insect breathing system could provide enough oxygen to fuel a flying insect as big as *Meganeura*.

Insects don't have lungs to suck oxygen out of the air, or blood to carry it to other parts of the body. Instead, insects breathe through holes in their bodies. The holes, called spiracles, are attached to hollow tubes, called tracheae (TRAY-kee-ay), that branch into and through the body. Air fills the tracheae, and the insect's cells absorb oxygen from the air.

However, the tracheae get narrower as they go farther into the body, and deliver less oxygen. Most scientists think that insect size is limited by how far the tracheae can carry oxygen and how quickly the cells can extract it. Today, the maximum size of an insect is much smaller than *Meganeura*.

So, how did *Meganeura* get so big, and how could it fly? The answers to both questions may lie with the Earth's atmosphere.

During the Carboniferous, the atmosphere contained far more oxygen than today. Nowadays, about 21 percent of the air we breathe is oxygen. *Meganeura*'s air contained as much as 35 percent oxygen. That means air could travel farther through *Meganeura*'s large body before the oxygen was used up.

Meganeura wasn't the only giant insect in the Carboniferous. There were also flies the size of small birds and millipedes longer than baseball bats. More oxygen could explain how all of them got so big.

This Brazilian dragonfly lived in the age of the dinosaurs. It's the first fossil dragonfly found that still shows color patterns.

Insects, like other animals, use oxygen to turn food into energy for growth. Researchers have been experimenting to see if more oxygen means bigger insects—and it seems to mean exactly that.

Fruit flies raised in an atmosphere of 23 percent oxygen—just a little higher than today's standard atmosphere—grew larger with every generation. The much higher oxygen level of *Meganeura*'s day could be the secret behind all the giants of the Carboniferous.

Oxygen also fuels muscle power. High levels of this gas in the atmosphere would deliver more oxygen to *Meganeura*'s flying muscles, giving them more strength and endurance. So, oxygen-rich air could also be the secret behind the mystery of *Meganeura* flight.

Like all dragonflies, this neon skimmer traps prey in a basket formed by its front two pairs of legs.

WHat FOSSILS CAN'T TELL US

FOSSILS TELL US WHAT the dragonfly giant looked like, but to see how it might have behaved we look at its modern cousins.

Dragonflies are mighty hunters. A dragonfly cruises through the air with its legs tucked forward, ready for action. When it spots prey, it swoops down and scoops the creature up with its first two pairs of legs, stuffs the victim in its mouth, and carries on hunting. One modern dragonfly was found with more than 100 mosquitoes in its mouth!

Meganeura probably hunted in the same way, preying on other flying insects and maybe even on small, slow-moving reptiles or amphibians.

DRAGONFLY FAMILY TIES

INSECTS WERE THE first creatures to grow wings and fly. It turned out to be a great idea.

Winged insects, called pterygotes (TAIR-I-gots), first appeared during the high-oxygen days of the Carboniferous period. They started subdividing into different groupings very quickly—and just kept subdividing. Since insects first developed wings, over 100 times more species of winged insects have existed than all species of flying reptiles, birds, and mammals combined.

Very early in their history, pterygotes settled into three large groups that survive today: the Ephemeroptera (mayflies), Neoptera (bugs, beetles, wasps, moths, flies, and a lot more), and Odonata. The Odonata are our friends the dragonflies and their close relatives, damselflies. Both *Meganeura* and all modern dragonflies are descended from those early Odonata.

The name Odonata comes from the Greek word for tooth and is usually translated as "toothed jaw." It refers to the adult's mouth, which has jagged edges that look almost like teeth.

Early Odonata developed many different strategies for making a living in the Carboniferous. One was to grow very big, like *Meganeura.* The extra-large dragonflies survived a long time—tens of millions of years, at least—but they couldn't survive the Permian Extinction of 250 million years ago.

A few groups of smaller dragonflies survived the terrible times of the Permian Extinction—and a good many disasters since then. Modern dragonflies and damselflies are the descendants of those survivors.

A green darner deposits her eggs in water, where they will hatch into water-dwelling nymphs. Darners are a large and widespread family of modern dragonflies.

As many as 5500 species of dragonfly and damselfly exist in the world today. They live everywhere except in the frozen areas of the Arctic and Antarctic, but they are most plentiful in tropical regions.

How can you tell a dragonfly from a damselfly? Damselflies are generally skinnier in the body than dragonflies and have different patterns of veins in their wings. Damselflies also have two sets of wings that are nearly equal in size. In dragonflies, the hind set of wings is broader than the front set.

WiNGLeSS Hunters

EVEN AS JUVENILES, DRAGONFLIES hunt for a living.

We think of dragonflies as flying insects, but they spend only a short part of their lives in the air. They spend much longer as wingless juveniles, called nymphs. The nymphs scoot around the bottoms of ponds and eat almost anything that comes within reach.

Nothing scares dragonfly nymphs! They've been known to catch and eat fish as big as they are.

As a nymph eats and grows, its outer covering gets too tight and cracks open. The nymph wriggles out, wearing a brand-new skin. This process is called molting. Each time it molts, the nymph is a little bigger and looks a little more like an adult. Some dragonfly nymphs eat and grow for a few months; others spend years in nymph form. Eventually, the nymph climbs out of the water, molts one last time, and emerges as an air-breathing, flying, adult dragonfly.

Meganeura nymphs probably grew like modern dragonfly nymphs, but it's hard to find the evidence. Animals that live in water rarely turn into fossils when they die. They're more likely to become dinner for another water creature.

A dragonfly nymph sits on a leaf just below the water's surface.

20

WHAT HAPPENED TO MEGANEURA?

THE LAST *MEGANEURA* DIED long ago, even before the age of dinosaurs. *Meganeura* fossils don't show up in rocks created less than about 250 million years ago. And that's an important clue.

Meganeura fossils disappear at the time of one of the greatest disasters to strike life on Earth—the Permian Extinction. The Permian period followed the Carboniferous and lasted from about 290 million years ago until 248 million years ago. Toward the end of the Permian, roughly 95 percent of all species on Earth went extinct—including all the giant insects.

What caused the extinction? Scientists have suggested several possibilities: huge lava flows that poisoned the air, a meteor strike, or changes in the sun. The most recent theory takes us back to *Meganeura*'s old friend, oxygen.

All through the Permian, oxygen levels in the atmosphere were declining. By the end of the Permian, the air was only 15 percent oxygen. That's like the air at the top of a very high mountain today—air so thin that a short walk would leave you gasping for breath. Animals such as *Meganeura*, adapted to air with more than twice as much oxygen, simply couldn't survive.

Even if it had lived through the Permian Extinction, *Meganeura* would have a tough time today, thanks to predators that didn't exist during the Carboniferous. Hawks and eagles, ravens and owls, cats, weasels, coyotes, raccoons, and a horde of other animals—all would happily make a meal of a giant dragonfly.

In our world, *Meganeura* wouldn't stand a chance!

21

WHEN DISASTER STRIKES

Life on Earth has traveled a bumpy road. Of all the species that have existed, more than 99 percent are now extinct. Most disappeared slowly and quietly, but some were unlucky. They were caught up in mass extinction events—terrible times when, for reasons we don't always understand, large numbers of species died off in a fairly short time.

Here are some of the major extinction events.

▶ **LATE PRECAMBRIAN EXTINCTION** (650 million years ago): About 70 percent of Precambrian life died, including almost all microorganisms. Possible cause: the most extensive glaciation Earth has ever known.

▶ **CAMBRIAN MASS EXTINCTION** (500 million years ago): Most animals died and 50 percent of animal families disappeared. Possible causes: glaciation, general cooling, lowering oxygen levels.

▶ **FINAL ORDOVICIAN EXTINCTION** (445 million years ago): Most life was in the sea, and most of it died. The extinction toll is estimated as high as 85 percent of species. Possible causes: glaciation, cooling sea temperatures, sea level drop.

▶ **DEVONIAN MASS EXTINCTION** (368 million years ago): Current evidence indicates that marine creatures were most seriously affected, but they were still the dominant form of animal life. As much as 70 to 80 percent of marine species were wiped out. Possible causes: dramatic cooling, meteorite impact, lowered oxygen levels.

22

► **PERMIAN EXTINCTION** (250 million years ago): The greatest mass extinction recorded in Earth's history—up to 90 percent of all species on the planet disappeared. Possible causes: meteorite impact, huge lava flows, massive release of poisonous gas, severe drop in oxygen content of air and oceans.

► **TRIASSIC-JURASSIC EXTINCTION** (200 million years ago): Perhaps half of known species went extinct, including many of the larger land creatures. This opened the way for dinosaurs to expand and dominate the planet. Possible causes: climate change, volcanic action, change in oxygen levels.

Tyrannosaurus rex is one of the most famous of extinct animals.

► **CRETACEOUS EXTINCTION** (65 million years ago): About 85 percent of all species on Earth died—including the dinosaurs. Probable cause: Most scientists agree the extinction was triggered by an asteroid that slammed into Earth.

23

Sarcosuchus imperator lounges on a riverbank 110 million years ago, while an ouranosaur herd browses nearby. The remains of both animals have been found in the same rock layers in Niger, West Africa.

3
croc-OH-DiLLY!

THE TÉNÉRÉ DESERT in northern Africa is a huge stretch of sand dunes, rock, and sun-baked ground.

But 110 million years ago, when dinosaurs ruled the Earth, the Ténéré was a wide green plain with lakes and a meandering river. Dinosaurs grazed on lush vegetation, insects and tiny mammals poked through the undergrowth, and turtles basked on the riverbank. Below the river's surface, giant fish swam—and a monster lurked.

There would have been no warning. One moment, a small dinosaur dipped its snout in the river for a drink. The next moment, the water erupted. Jaws as long as a full-grown human clamped down on the dinosaur's head and neck. A massive, muscular body dragged the victim into the river where the hunter could kill and eat it at leisure.

24

The hunter was *Sarcosuchus imperator,* nicknamed SuperCroc. And it was huge. A full-grown adult was as long as a city bus and as heavy as a small whale.

WALKING ON
CROCODILE SKULLS

CROCODILES, ALLIGATORS, AND ALL their ancestors and relatives, going back more than 200 million years, are commonly called crocodilians—partly because it's shorter and easier to say than the more correct term, crocodylomorpha!

There have been a lot of crocodilians, but *Sarcosuchus* (sar-koh-SYU-kus) may have been the biggest of all.

We know a lot about *Sarcosuchus* because so many of its bones have survived. They were buried in muddy river sediments, along with the bones of other creatures of the time. Then the climate changed, the river dried up, and sediment turned to stone, sealing in the remains of *Sarcosuchus*'s world.

The bones lay undisturbed for millions of years. Then, in the 1960s, French

25

The modern saltwater crocodile looks much like its ancient relatives.

Croc-oh-Dilly!

paleontologists studying a collection of fossils found by an expedition to the Ténéré realized that a partial skull and some bones belonged to a very large crocodilian. They named it *Sarcosuchus imperator,* which means "flesh crocodile emperor."

In 1997, an American paleontologist looking for dinosaur fossils spotted a huge crocodile jaw embedded in the desert's rocky floor and recognized it as *Sarcosuchus.* He returned with a team of researchers to dig up fossils of the animal they nicknamed SuperCroc.

The researchers found more than they expected. Near the giant jawbone was a line of vertebrae from the animal's spine. Not far away, they found more skulls and bones—a treasure trove of *Sarcosuchus* fossils. There were so many, the researchers said, that they were walking across crocodile skulls as they worked.

The team found partial skeletons from five different animals, including skulls, vertebrae, limb bones, teeth, and large bony scales called scutes that form a crocodile's armor. Some of the scutes were as big as a school notebook and much thicker. Altogether, they had about half of a SuperCroc skeleton—enough to get a clear idea of what *Sarcosuchus* looked like.

Teeth, teeth, and more teeth

SARCOSUCHUS HAD A TYPICAL crocodilian shape: short legs, a long, low body and flattened skull, a muscular tail, and a long, toothy snout. Like all modern crocodiles, its main sense organs were on top of its skull. That allowed it to float with only its eyes, ears, and nostrils above water, waiting for animals to ambush.

It was well equipped for an ambush. *Sarcosuchus's* jaws were lined with more than 130 teeth, round and pointed like thick spikes and as long as a grown-up's finger. SuperCroc could have delivered a super bite!

A Florida researcher estimated how strong its bite might have been by

SuperCroc had a bulge on its snout, much like the bulla on the snout of this male gharial.

measuring the bite force of modern alligators. The answer: more than 8000 kilograms (18,000 pounds) of force. That estimate might be high, since *Sarcosuchus* had a narrower jaw design than alligators. Still, trying to pry open SuperCroc's jaws would be like trying to lift an elephant.

What sorts of animals were likely to be on the wrong end of SuperCroc's bite? Fish as long as a bathtub swam in the river, and dinosaurs and turtles lived on the banks. *Sarcosuchus* might have dined on any of them.

Sarcosuchus had one puzzling oddity. On the end of its snout was an inflatable, bowl-shaped structure called a bulla. The Indian gharial, a modern fish-eating crocodile, has a similar structure—but only on the males. All of the *Sarcosuchus* skulls found so far, male and female, have shown signs of a bulla. The structure might have improved the croc's sense of smell or it might have made the animal's calls louder. Or perhaps it served some other purpose altogether.

27

FUN FACTS

Crocodiles are noisy! They grunt, growl, bark, bellow, hiss, squeak, roar, and even make a popping noise by slapping their jaws against the water.

One African village lives peacefully beside a pond full of Nile crocodiles. The villagers believe the crocodiles are linked with their ancestors, so they feed them and keep the pond full of water. In return, the crocodiles rarely bite villagers—and only when provoked!

Crocodilians have the most powerful bite for their size in the modern animal world, more than twice as strong as the runner-up species, the spotted hyena.

When a crocodile's mouth is closed, you can still see its upper and lower teeth.

The American alligator was almost wiped out a century ago to feed the demand for alligator-leather handbags and boots. Now hunting the big reptiles is strictly controlled, alligator leather comes from alligator farms, and there are millions of wild American alligators.

How can you tell a crocodile from an alligator? Alligators have wide snouts, and when their mouths are closed, the teeth in the lower jaw can't be seen. Crocodiles have narrower snouts, and two large teeth near the front of the lower jaw stick out when their mouths are closed.

Crocodilians live as far north as the Yangtze River in China, and as far south as South Africa and Australia. They even survive in ponds in the Sahara desert.

HOW DID SARCOSUCHUS GET SO BIG?

IF HUMAN BABIES GREW as fast as modern croc babies, you'd be as tall as a basketball player before you started school. But no crocodile today gets as big as *Sarcosuchus imperator*—and SuperCroc wasn't the only ancient giant. *Deinosuchus,* an alligator-like creature that lived about 80 million years ago in North America, was probably as big or even bigger.

A study of *Deinosuchus's* scutes suggests a possible explanation for the size of giant crocodilians. Crocodilian scutes have growth rings that can provide information about the animal's age and how quickly it grew—although the growth rings aren't as clear as the growth rings in trees.

Scutes of modern crocodilians show that they grow quickly until they reach adult size. Then their growth rate slows down.

Deinosuchus's scutes show no sign that the growth rate slowed. Some scientists believe that giant crocodilians like *Deinosuchus* and *Sarcosuchus* simply grew at full speed, all their lives.

Bony plates called scutes protect the crocodile's back and tail—and give scientists information about an animal's growth.

STILL HANGING AROUND

CROCODILIANS HAVE BEEN AROUND for at least 230 million years. They've lived on land, in water, in swamps and marshes. They've eaten insects, land animals, fish, even plants.

Modern crocodilians are less varied than their relatives of long ago. About two dozen species survive today. They all live in or near water in the warmth of the tropics and subtropics, and they all eat meat.

The largest living crocodile is *Crocodylus porosus*—commonly called the estuarine crocodile, the saltwater crocodile, or the saltie. A large proportion of the world's wild population of salties lives in Australia. Salties have been known to swim long distances at sea, but they're also comfortable in the fresh water of rivers and inland lakes.

The saltwater crocodile is big. Measured by mass, it's the world's largest reptile (although some snakes are longer). But even a record-size saltie would be little more than half the length of *Sarcosuchus* and only about a sixth of its weight.

Like Nothing Else on Earth

THERE'S NOTHING IN the animal kingdom quite like crocodilians.

Take, for example, their hearts. All other reptiles have three-chambered hearts. Crocs have four-chambered hearts, like birds and mammals—but with a twist. Croc hearts have valves that can close off one side of the heart and send used blood back through the croc's body instead of into its lungs to gather more oxygen. Some scientists think this system helps the croc conserve oxygen during long dives.

Crocodilians also have strange heads. A plate of solid bone separates the croc's nasal passages from its mouth, so it can breathe through its nostrils at the water surface even when its mouth is full of water.

When it dives, a crocodilian closes a flap of skin at the back of its throat to stop water entering its lungs. Other flaps of skin protect its nostrils and ears, and a transparent third eyelid slides across the croc's eyes.

From their necks to halfway down their tails, crocodilians' backs are covered with armor—thick, interlocking bony scutes that are part of their skin.

30

Beneath the armor is an extra-strong spine, which helps crocodilians support their weight on land or twist and turn in the water.

Even with heavy armor and reinforced skeletons, crocs suffer injuries, but they rarely get infections. Their blood has antibiotic properties so effective that medical researchers are studying it in search of new medicines.

BUMPS THAT CAN SEE IN THE NIGHT

ONE OF THE STRANGEST things about crocodilians is their sixth sense.

If you look at a picture of an American alligator, you'll see dark bumps on its jaw, almost like beard stubble. All living crocodilians have similar bumps, sometimes over their entire bodies and even inside their mouths.

The dark bumps are pressure sensors that operate only where air and water meet. And they're amazingly sensitive. An experiment with baby alligators

The black spots on the alligator's jaw sense even a tiny change in water pressure.

showed that the little animals could sense a single drop of water splashing into their tank—even with the lights off and their ears temporarily blocked. If the bumps on their jaws were covered, however, they didn't react to water drops.

The bumps are so sensitive that crocodilians can locate an animal that disturbs the water's surface even in the black of night—usually before the animal realizes a croc is nearby.

Sarcosuchus may have been able do the same thing. The sensors leave holes in the bone where their nerve bundles connect to the central nervous system. These holes have been found in fossils of extinct crocodilians, but only in species such as SuperCroc that lived and hunted at the water's surface.

CROCODILIAN FAMILY TIES

A saltwater crocodile suns itself on a log, with its mouth open to get rid of extra heat.

SARCOSUCHUS AND LIVING crocodilians are both descendants of the archosaurs (AR-koh-sors). So are dinosaurs and birds. Archosaurs—the name means "ruling reptiles"—first appeared in the late Permian, more than 250 million years ago. By the Mesozoic era, they were the dominant animals on land, and some even took to the seas.

The archosaurs subdivided into three major groups: pterosaurs, dinosaurs, and crocodilians. Pterosaurs were flying reptiles, long extinct. Dinosaurs became extinct about 65 million years ago, leaving their descendants, the birds. Crocodilians split off from the archosaurs as much as 230 million years ago, and they're still around today.

Over that long period of time, there have been hundreds of crocodilian species—also called crocodyliforms—in dozens of subgroups. *Sarcosuchus* belonged to one subgroup that died out long ago.

All living crocodilians and their extinct ancestors belong to a different subgroup. In 2005, fossils of the oldest known direct ancestor of modern crocs were found in Australia. The little animal, barely as long as a walking stick, lived 98 to 95 million years ago.

Why aren't there any crocodilians as big as *Sarcosuchus* today? One possible reason is that mammals—including humans—dominate the planet now and use most of its resources. It takes a lot of food over a lot of years for a crocodile to grow as big as *Sarcosuchus*, and that much food just isn't available to modern crocodiles.

Another possible reason is that crocodiles no longer need to grow as big as *Sarcosuchus*. The giant crocodilian competed with dinosaurs and hunted giant fish. Modern crocodiles don't have to deal with giants, so they don't need to be giants themselves.

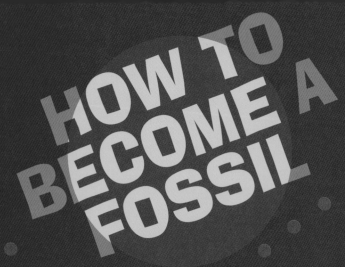
HOW TO BECOME A FOSSIL

If you want to become a fossil, here are a few things to think about:

▶ A good first step is to be a crocodile. A crocodile skull is reinforced with extra bone to give the animal a stronger bite. That means it has a better chance than most skulls of lasting long enough, unbroken, to make a good fossil.

▶ If you can't arrange to be a crocodile, at least try to be something with strong bones and teeth. Those are the bits that tend to survive long enough to become fossils.

▶ It's also important to die in the right place. The bodies of most animals are torn apart by scavengers. Then insects, fungi, bacteria, and weathering eventually turn the bones and other leftovers into dust.

▶ The best place for a future fossil to die is where something will cover the body before it has a chance to decay. Many of the best fossils have been covered by volcanic ash, ocean-floor sand, or stream sediment such as sand or mud.

▶ It's also important that the layers of ash or sediment continue to build up and protect your body from the air. After a long time—thousands of years or more—minerals will seep into your bones and teeth, preserving them. Or the space left by your body after it disintegrates will fill with other minerals, creating a cast of your original body or bones.

34

This fish died in the right place to become a fossil. Details of its bones and spines are preserved in the rock that formed around the fish's body.

► The next thing a good fossil needs is a process that will expose it to the air again without destroying it. In Canada's Alberta Badlands, rivers cut through sediments deposited over millions of years to expose generations of dinosaur bones. In Africa's Ténéré Desert, the wind does the same job.

► Finally, your fossil has to be found. It helps to be somewhere accessible, a place where a person might pass by, see the fossil, and recognize what it is. That might be the most difficult coincidence of all!

Aepycamelus was an ancient giraffe-like camel that once lived in North America.

THE CAMEL'S INTERRUPTED JOURNEY 4

SIXTY-FIVE MILLION YEARS AGO, Earth suffered a cosmic accident. Something enormous—a comet or an asteroid—hurtled out of space and slammed into the planet where eastern Mexico is now.

The impact lit huge fires around the globe. Dust and gas filled the skies, the clouds poured acid rain, and more than half the species of animals on Earth perished—including all the dinosaurs.

But life itself survived, and new animals evolved to fill the spaces left by the dead. Twenty-five million years later, the world was again full of living things, with a new dominant group—the mammals.

Among them was *Protylopus* (pro-TILL-oh-puss), a four-legged mammal about the size of a hare. *Protylopus* lived in North America, skittering through the forest undergrowth and browsing on leaves. It had a long neck, a narrow head, and four toes on each small foot. If you saw it, you'd never recognize what it was—a camel.

Wait a minute! What's an ancient camel doing in North America?

First Steps
on the
Journey

STRANGE AS IT SEEMS NOW, camels originated in North America. *Protylopus* is the first camel-like creature in the fossil record, but not the last, and most of them lived in North America.

Protylopus's world was warm and covered with thick forests. But as North America got cooler and drier, the forests gave way to open woods and grasslands—a bonanza for plant-eaters. Grass is more nutritious than tree or shrub leaves, so many plant-eaters switched to grass and flourished. They multiplied, splintered into new species, and grew bigger. A lot bigger.

Camelids—a term that includes all members of the family—were no exception. Over tens of millions of years, they got bigger, more numerous, more varied, and spread into almost every habitat in North America.

One group, called the giraffe-camels, stuck close to woodlands. They weren't related to giraffes, but they developed long giraffe-like legs and necks, and browsed the branches of trees above the reach of other plant-eaters. *Aepycamelus* was the largest of them. Its head, atop a long, S-shaped neck, reached as high as a basketball hoop.

Giraffe-camels died out more than 5 million years ago, but other camelids survived and prospered. A bewildering array of camel species evolved, lived, and died in North America. They ranged in size from little gazelle-like creatures to the giant camel, *Titanotylopus* (tie-tan-oh-TILL-oh-puss). It was big enough to stand on the ground outside a modern house and peek into the second-story window.

37

FUN Facts

Camels grind their teeth—and it's good for them! Camels' teeth keep growing throughout their lives, so grinding them together helps keep the teeth the right length.

The two-humped Bactrian camel and the one-humped dromedary are usually considered separate species. However, one-humped camels actually have a small second hump in front of their main hump, and some scientists think the two camels are just variations of the same species. To complicate the picture further, Bactrian camels and dromedaries can interbreed, so plenty of camels are a mix of the two types.

Camels' teeth never stop growing.

The vicuña's coat produces the finest wool in the world, less than half as thick as the finest sheep's wool. During the time of the Inca empire, vicuña wool was reserved for royalty and commoners were forbidden to wear it.

The Bridge of 23 Camels in Lillooet, British Columbia, commemorates the time, in 1862, when a businessman imported 23 camels to haul freight on the Cariboo Gold Rush trails. Unfortunately, the camels terrified horses, ate everything they could reach, including hats and bars of soap, and had to wear canvas boots to protect their feet. After less than a year, the businessman gave up on camels.

The remains of one of the last large North American camels—*Camelops hesternus*, known as the western camel or yesterday's camel—have been found in locations as far apart as California and the Yukon.

Camels are famous for spitting when they're annoyed or threatened. But that's not saliva. If a camel spits on you, you're getting a sample of its stomach contents.

The earliest members of the camel family may have looked like small versions of this South American guanaco.

TWISTS IN THE ROAD

FOR 35 MILLION YEARS, camelids evolved and adapted without ever leaving North America. And with good reason. During most of that time, North America was an island continent, surrounded by ocean.

About 5 million years ago, things changed. Sea levels dropped, exposing a strip of dry land between Alaska and Siberia. Camels and other animals crossed to Asia and on into Europe. The camelids that migrated to Asia gave rise to modern camels—large, long-legged animals with long, S-shaped necks and fatty humps on their backs.

A couple of million years later, the rising land of Central America finally linked North and South America, and a different group of camelids headed south. Their living descendants are two wild species, the guanaco and the vicuña, and two domestic species, the alpaca and the llama. All are smaller than camels, with straighter necks and no humps.

Leaving home, it turned out, was the best thing camelids could have done. In North America, they were doomed—but not right away.

39

For hundreds of thousands of years, during the last part of the most recent ice age, huge ice sheets advanced and retreated across northern North America. Camelids survived the ice, growing thick coats for warmth and eating whatever food was available. Finally, only about 12,000 years ago, the ice sheets retreated and kept on retreating.

Then, just when it seemed that the worst was over, the last North American camel died. Camels were extinct on their home continent.

THE JOURNEY almost ends

THE ONCE GREAT CAMEL family was in deep trouble. All that remained were a couple of llama-like species in the mountains of South America and one or two species of camel in Asia.

Strange as it seems, what may have saved them from extinction is humankind.

Camels provide transportation in some of the most inhospitable places. This salt caravan is crossing the Ténéré Desert in Africa.

Long ago, people discovered that camels and llamas are useful. As the number of wild camelids dwindled, the number of animals in domestic herds increased.

In South America, the Incas domesticated camelids as much as 7000 years ago, using them for meat, wool, and transportation.

In Asia, people used camels for similar purposes. The two-humped Bactrian camel was domesticated at least 4500 years ago, and the one-humped dromedary, 5000 or more years ago. Camels have provided milk, meat, wool, and transportation ever since. And camel dung is so dry that people use it as fuel for fires!

WHat Makes it a CAMeL?

CAMELIDS HAVE BEEN WILD and tame, as small as a hare or almost as big as an elephant. They've lived in forests, prairies, mountains, deserts, and tundra. They've had two humps, one hump, and no humps at all. What do they have in common?

One thing is their shape. Camelids all have long, slender necks, narrow heads that are mostly muzzle, long legs, and no horns.

Another common camelid feature is the three-chambered stomach. Camelids are ruminants—plant-eaters with multi-chambered stomachs that digest their food in stages. First, a ruminant swallows the raw material. Later, it forces a wad of partially digested food, called the cud, back into its mouth for more chewing. Then it swallows the cud to finish the digestion process in another part of the stomach. Most ruminants, like the cow, have four stomach chambers. Camelids are the only ruminants with just three stomach chambers.

LOCO MOTION!

UNUSUAL FEET AND A STRANGE WAY of walking also make camelids distinct from other animals.

Camelids are even-toed ungulates, hoofed mammals with an even number of toes on each foot. In the case of camelids, the number of toes is two—and that's been true for at least 30 million years.

Most ungulates walk on the tips of their toes, on hooves that evolved from claws. Animals such as deer have "split hooves"—actually two hooves side by side. The two long bones leading to the hooves are fused into a single bone called the cannon bone.

Camelid feet are different. The cannon bone is only partly fused. Near the foot, it separates into two bones again, and the toes spread outward. Instead of hooves, camelid toes have wide leathery pads on the bottom and flattened claws like thick toenails on top. When a camel puts weight on its foot, the toes flatten against the ground and the leathery pads spread out to make a wide surface that stops the foot from sinking into soft earth or sand.

Camelids have a peculiar walk too. Other four-footed animals move the legs on opposite corners of their bodies at the same time. A dog or a horse will move its right front leg forward together with its left hind leg. That means that one leg on each side provides support while the other legs move.

The camel's walk is called pacing. The legs on the left side of the body move forward together; then both legs on the right side of the body move forward. As a result, the camel rocks from side to side as it moves. Fossil footprints of *Poebrotherium* (poh-bro-THEER-ee-um), a goat-sized camel that lived 30 million years ago, show that it walked, and rocked, like a modern camel.

42

CAMELID FAMILY TIES

Bactrian camels, from the steppes of eastern Asia, have two humps.

THE CAMELID FAMILY TREE is fairly clear—except for the beginning.

Tiny leaf-eater *Protylopus* is separated from modern camels by 40 million years. That's not long compared to crocodiles or dragonflies, but it's long enough that the fossil record doesn't provide much information about the early part. Currently, some scientists think *Protylopus* was a direct ancestor of all camelids and some think it was a relative of that direct ancestor.

A few million years after *Protylopus*, things get a bit clearer. Around 30 million years ago, the camel family was represented by goat-sized *Poebrotherium*. It looked like a larger version of *Protylopus*, but it ate grass as well as leaves.

After *Poebrotherium*'s time, the camel family split into three branches. Two of them have died out: the giraffe-camels and a group that looked a bit like gazelles. Modern camelids are descended from the third group, the protolabine camels.

Protolabine camels were named for *Protolabis* (proh-toh-LAY-bis), a llama-sized animal that lived 12 million years ago. Two major lines of camelid evolution split off from *Protolabis*. One led eventually to the two species of camel that survive today—the Bactrian camel and the dromedary. The other led to the South American camelids—the guanaco, vicuña, llama, and alpaca.

The Australian outback is a dry and dangerous place, but large numbers of camels live there in the wild.

TOUGHING it out

CAMELS ARE EXPERTS at making the best of a bad situation. That's how they survive so well in deserts.

Many people think that a camel stores water in its hump. Actually, the hump is mainly fat that the camel's body can use when food is scarce. When a camel has plenty of food, its hump gets bigger. When food is hard to find, the hump gets smaller and often slumps to one side.

Camels can't go without water entirely, but they can go for long periods without drinking. They get most of the water they need from the plants they eat. Plants that grow in dry places such as deserts are good at trapping and holding whatever water is available. Also, the camel's body doesn't waste water. Its droppings have so little water in them that they can be used as fuel for a campfire as soon as they come out of the camel!

When a camel finally gets to a waterhole, it can drink a quarter of its weight's worth of water in one session. That amount of water would kill most animals, but camels have special red blood cells that can swell up with fluid to almost two and a half times their normal size without bursting.

44

THe PaTH oF THe DROMeDaRy

WHEN WE THINK OF a camel, we usually picture the one-humped dromedary or Arabian camel. It's tall, with gangly legs and a short string of a tail.

Dromedaries have served humans for a long time. They carried silks and spices from China to Europe a thousand years ago. They carried salt across the deserts of North Africa. They carried Persian archers, Roman soldiers, Arab warriors, and troops from both sides in the First and Second World Wars.

Today dromedaries are the most plentiful camelid in the world—but they're extinct in the wild. Nowhere in the world is there a dromedary population that hasn't, at some point, passed through human hands. But not all modern dromedaries live in domestic herds.

Occasionally, groups of camels have been abandoned or have escaped from human control. They are "feral" animals, rather than wild animals—which means they come from domestic stock, even though they now live in the wild.

The world's largest group of feral dromedaries lives on an island continent, just as their North American ancestors did, but on the other side of the world—Australia.

Camels were brought to Australia in the mid-1800s to transport goods in the outback. When machinery took over the work, many of the camels were turned loose. They discovered that Australia

suited them just fine, and they multiplied. No one knows exactly how many camels roam the Australian outback, but estimates run from 80,000 to a million or more.

So, despite everything, camelids survive. And they owe it to humans!

45

Brightly colored blankets and harnessing show how much their human owners value these sleek domestic dromedaries.

The Camel's Interrupted Journey

MORE CLUES TO THE PAST

Fossilized animals aren't the only clues to the ancient past. Information can be found in trees, rocks, ice, and muck, in mountains and in microscopic grains of pollen. Scientists are finding more and more ways to reveal the history of life on Earth.

▶ **TRACKWAYS:** The footprints of ancient animals are sometimes preserved when materials such as mud, wet sand, or volcanic ash turn to stone. Fossil trackways can tell us how tall and heavy an animal was, how it walked, whether it dragged its tail or carried it off the ground, and whether it traveled with other animals or on its own.

▶ **GENETIC CODES:** Fossil bones and other ancient substances sometimes still contain genetic material, such as DNA. By analyzing the genetic material, we can learn a great deal, including how animals are related to each other and to modern animals, how populations change and move around, and whether similar-looking animals belong to the same or different species.

Ancient leaves left imprints in the rocks of Svalbard, an island in the Arctic where no trees grow today.

▶ **GEOLOGY:** The rock layers in which a fossil is found contain information about when the animal lived, what happened before and after it lived, and what kind of landscape it lived in. A vital clue to the cause of the Cretaceous Extinction that killed the dinosaurs was a thin layer of clay rich in iridium and platinum, rare elements on Earth but common in meteorites.

47

▶ **ICE CORES:** Ice in glaciers and icefields can be hundreds of thousands of years old. It's laid down year after year in layers that trap such things as dust, pollen, ash from forest fires and volcanoes, and even bubbles of ancient atmosphere. Scientists drill down through thousands of years of frozen water, pull up a long column of ice—an ice core—and study it to fill in our record of the past.

More Clues to the Past

The giant ground sloth, *Eremotherium*, stands on its hind legs to reach the leaves at the top of a tree.

5

SIZE ISN'T
EVERYTHING

IT WAS A HOT, SUNNY DAY in the southern Caribbean about 8 million years ago. To the south lay the continent of South America. In the west, wisps of smoke marked where the volcanoes of Central America were gradually rising from the sea. Waves splashed against the rocky shores of islands that punctuated the open ocean between North and South America.

A raft of tangled vegetation rocked on the waves, drifting northward. On it sprawled a large, hairy beast—damp, bedraggled, and slightly puzzled. It was a giant ground sloth and it was about to discover North America.

Well, maybe it didn't happen quite that way. But it could have.

Ground sloths were among the first large South American animals to migrate to North America—and they did it while the two continents were still separate. North and South America weren't permanently joined by dry land until the Isthmus of Panama formed about 3 million years ago.

Scientists suggest that the large plant-eaters could have floated on vegetation mats, drifting northward from island to island until they reached the southern shores of North America. Floating islands of intertwined vegetation are still common in shallow lakes and wetlands in many parts of the world, including Panama, and sometimes storms or tides wash them out to sea, along with the plants and animals living on them.

Once the ground sloths arrived in North America, they made themselves at home and spread across most of the continent. When the Panamanian land bridge finally formed, even more sloths joined them. Until about 11,000 years ago, at least 19 species of sloth lived in the Americas, from near the southern tip of South America to north of the Arctic Circle.

And then they were gone—all but a few small, inconspicuous sloths that spend their lives hanging from the branches of trees. What went wrong?

Specialists in Size

IF SIZE ALONE COULD KEEP an animal safe, we'd be living in a world full of sloths. Take *Eremotherium eomigrans* (air-eh-moh-THEER-ee-um ee-oh-MY-granz), for example. One of the largest of the North American ground sloths, it was almost unimaginably big.

Picture a creature at least as huge and heavy as an elephant, but covered in long, coarse hair. Rearing up on its hind legs—which it often did—*Eremotherium* would have been taller than three men standing on each other's shoulders. Its head was mostly jaw—a massive, muscled jaw that could grind up the toughest vegetation. Measured from the tip of its long muscular tail to its blunt nose, the sloth was as long as a pickup truck.

On its front feet, *Eremotherium* had four thick, curved claws. The longest

were the length of bread knives. Scientists think the sloth probably used its claws to hook tree branches and pull them within reach of its mouth, or to dig up roots.

Its hind feet had large claws too, and all those claws forced the sloth to walk in a very peculiar way. It put its weight on the outer sides of its front paws, with the claws turned inward. On the hind feet, the weight rested on a combination of the outer side of the foot and a large heart-shaped pad below the third and fourth claws.

Despite this awkward gait, *Eremotherium* covered a lot of territory. Its fossils have been found from Brazil to the southern United States.

An even bigger sloth, *Megatherium americanum,* lived in South America and possibly as far north as Texas. Like *Eremotherium,* it could stand upright, and fossil footprints show it could walk on its hind legs.

Megatherium had just three claws on its front paws. South American researchers who have studied the shape of *Megatherium*'s front limbs think it could have used its claws like knives to stab prey. They suspect the giant sloth might have become a meat-eater when the climate dried and plants became scarcer.

50

FUN Facts

At some times of the year, tree sloths turn greenish. That's because algae living in the grooves of their hairs turn green during the rainy season.

Three-toed tree sloths have extra-long, extra-flexible necks that allow them to twist their heads in three-quarters of a circle and look forward even when they're hanging upside-down.

As much as two-thirds of a sloth's weight is the contents of its stomach.

Several species of moth, tick, and beetle live permanently in the hair of tree sloths.

A tree sloth looks down from the safety of a high branch.

Sloths belong to an order that used to be called edentates, which means "toothless." The name was changed because almost all members of the order, including sloths, have teeth!

As recently as 1994, an expedition searched Brazilian forests in the hope of finding a surviving giant ground sloth. None was found.

Giant ground sloths had peglike side teeth and sharp cutting teeth that never stopped growing. Chewing tough vegetation kept them worn down.

Strange Clues to Strange Beasts

WE KNOW A LOT ABOUT giant ground sloths because they left so much evidence behind. There are fossil bones and teeth, of course, including entire skeletons of some species. But ground sloths left other clues as well.

Many species spent time in caves—and caves are good at preserving the past. In the cold, dry caves of Argentina, people have found bones with bits of dried flesh still clinging to them and even pieces of the animal's hide, covered with coarse hair. Small armor plates, like bony coins, were embedded in the skin to make the tough hide even tougher.

Some of the best evidence about how and when sloths lived comes from coprolites. That's just a nice, clean, scientific term for sloth dung! Coprolites have been preserved in caves in both South America and North America. One cave in Arizona seems to have been used as a toilet by generations of Shasta ground sloths (*Nothrotheriops shastensis*), the last giant ground sloths to survive in North America.

So, what can you learn from dung? Lots!

By analyzing coprolites, you can figure out what an animal ate. Researchers have identified more than 70 kinds of plants in coprolites from that Arizona cave. They even know when the plants were eaten—between 40,000 years ago and 11,000 years ago. And the range of plants tells us what the climate was like. Scientists have also developed ways to retrieve genetic information from coprolites—not just the sloth's genetic information, but the genetic codes of the plants as well.

This 11,000-year-old dung was left by a Shasta ground sloth in Rampart Cave, Arizona.

52

In this group portrait, Jefferson's ground sloth is on the far left, and *Eremotherium* is on the right, at the back. The large sloth in front is *Paramylodon*, and the smallest is the Shasta ground sloth.

A PRESIDENTIAL ANIMAL

NOT ALL THE GROUND SLOTHS were giants. One of the most famous, Jefferson's ground sloth, was the size of a large bear. It was named for the American president, Thomas Jefferson, who was a respected scientist and an early paleontologist.

Jefferson was fascinated by fossils and prehistoric animals. In 1797, four years before he became president, he made a presentation to the American Philosophical Society describing a fossil creature that he called *Megalonyx*, or "large-clawed." Later it was named *Megalonyx jeffersonii* in his honor.

Jefferson's ground sloth was once the most widespread sloth in North America. Its bones have been found above the Arctic Circle and as far south as central Mexico. Jefferson himself thought the animals might still be alive somewhere. When he became president, he sent the explorers Lewis and Clark west to find a water route across the continent—and also asked them to keep an eye open for *Megalonyx*.

But Lewis and Clark were several thousand years too late.

53

Last of the GROUND Sloths

GROUND SLOTHS DIED OUT long ago. How long? And what killed them? Those are important questions for our understanding of extinctions.

The last North American ground sloths died 11,000 years ago, and a few centuries later the South American ground sloths were gone. However, some small species of *Megalonyx* ground sloths may have survived longer on a few Caribbean islands.

A study of sloth bones in Cuba, Haiti, the Dominican Republic, and Puerto Rico shows that some of the animals may have died as recently as 5000 years ago. Other evidence shows that humans first settled the islands at roughly that time.

Did humans kill the sloths? That's one theory. Sloths died out in North and South America about the time that the human population expanded across those two continents. So far, however, no one has found clear evidence of hunting—such as a spear point stuck in a sloth bone or bones that show signs of having been cut up for human consumption.

A tree sloth is wedged, secure and comfortable, into the crook of a tree.

SLOTH FAMILY TIES

GIANT GROUND SLOTHS and living tree sloths have strange relatives too. They belong to a group of South American mammals called the xenarthrans (zen-ARTH-rans). The other members of the group are armadillos and anteaters.

It's hard to see how animals that look so different from each other could be close relatives. However, under the skin they have a few important things in common.

One thing is their lower backbones. Xenarthra means "strange joint" and refers to the odd, interlocking vertebrae they all share. It's a design that's particularly useful for supporting a shell—and that might mean that all of these strange animals are descended from shelled ancestors.

The xenarthrans also have fewer and simpler teeth than most other mammals. In the case of some anteaters, the teeth have disappeared altogether. Sloths and armadillos have simple peglike teeth. The teeth don't have the hard enamel coating that protects most mammal teeth, so they wear down quickly. However, to compensate, xenarthran teeth keep growing throughout the animal's life.

Sloths and their relatives are a very old order, one of the earliest groups of mammals to appear in South America. The oldest xenarthran fossils found so far belonged to an armadillo-like creature that lived 60 million years ago. The earliest sloth fossils were found in deposits laid down in the Oligocene epoch, perhaps 30 million years ago.

A baby sloth snuggles in its mother's fur.

The fossil record for ground sloths is good, since many of them lived in cool, dry grasslands where their bones were preserved. Unfortunately, it's difficult to determine precisely which of the ancient ground sloths are most closely related to living tree sloths. The problem: there is no fossil record at all for tree sloths. That's not surprising. Animals that live in forests rarely leave fossils. Predators, insects, bacteria, and the soil itself break down the flesh and bone until nothing is left.

SPECIALIZING IN INVISIBILITY

GROWING REALLY BIG didn't protect ground sloths from extinction. The handful of remaining sloth species has taken a different approach, and it seems to be working. Modern sloths are small, slow, and almost invisible.

Two groups of sloths survive today: two-toed sloths and three-toed sloths. All of them spend their lives high in the trees of South and Central American forests, living slow, quiet lives among the leaves.

Two-toed sloths have two toes on their front feet and three on their back feet, while three-toed sloths have three toes on each foot. The two-toed sloths are a little larger—about the size of a long-legged raccoon. Otherwise, the two kinds of sloth look much alike—small, blunt heads, shaggy coats, and gangly legs that end in long, hooked claws.

And all of them are odd.

The tree sloth's shaggy hair grows from its belly toward its back—the opposite direction from other animals. However, the direction makes sense for sloths. Since they spend most of their lives hanging upside down from branches, their upside-down hair is actually right-side up—especially for shedding rain!

This sloth travels by hooking its curved claws over a branch.

56

The sloths' long, curved claws allow them to hang from branches with almost no effort. They just hook their claws over a branch and dangle. When they're not dangling from a branch, sloths are likely to be wedged into a fork of the tree, dozing. They sleep or rest as much as 20 hours a day.

Tree sloths spend very little time on the ground. The green in this sloth's coat shows where colonies of algae live.

Low-ENERGY Life

SLOTHS LIVE VERY, VERY SLOWLY. They move slowly, digest slowly, and think slowly. Sloths simply can't afford to waste energy.

Their main source of food is leaves—and leaves don't provide much nutrition. The little energy they contain is locked into a tough, almost indigestible material called cellulose. Bacteria are just about the only thing that can break down cellulose, so sloths have large colonies of bacteria living in their digestive tracts.

Even with the help of bacteria, sloth digestion is slow. Food makes its way through a human's digestive system in about a day. Sloths digest their meals for a month or more, and they poop only about once a week. When they do feel the need, sloths climb all the way down to the ground and use the same spot again and again. This is a dangerous time for sloths. Their leg muscles are designed for climbing and hanging, not for walking, so they have to crawl when they're on the ground. That makes them vulnerable to predators.

Fortunately, very few predators are interested in them. Harpy eagles will eat sloth if they get a chance, and so will jaguars. But most of the time sloths hang quietly in trees, their mottled fur blending in with the background of leaves and branches—and predators simply don't see them.

57

Size Isn't Everything

WHERE DID ALL THE GIANTS GO?

About 14,000 years ago, near the end of the last ice age in an epoch called the Pleistocene (PLICE-toh-seen), the Americas were home to some of the largest and strangest land mammals that have ever lived: mammoths and mastodons, giant camels, huge ground sloths, glyptodonts, giant short-faced bears, saber-tooth cats, lions, dire wolves, and more.

BY 10,000 YEARS AGO, almost all of them had disappeared from the Americas. The loss of those animals has become known as the Great Pleistocene Die-off—and what caused it is a subject of hot debate.

At least two important things happened around that time. The glaciers retreated, changing the landscape and environment dramatically. And humans spread through the Americas. Could one of those changes have killed off so many animals? Or both? Or something else?

58

Here are the two major theories currently being debated:

▶ **THE OVERKILL HYPOTHESIS:** Exactly when people first arrived in the Americas is uncertain—and very controversial. However, it's clear that a human population explosion took place in the Americas as the last ice age ended. The tools from that time show that the humans were skilled hunters with first-rate stone and bone weapons. According to the overkill hypothesis, the hunters found a paradise of large mammals and hunted them to the point where the populations could no longer survive.

▶ THE CLIMATE CHANGE HYPOTHESIS: The climate was warming at the end of the Pleistocene. Glaciers melted into vast lakes, silty rivers cut new paths through the landscape, and vegetation changed as patterns of rainfall and wind shifted. The transformation was dramatic, and it happened quickly. Perhaps too quickly. Many animals that had evolved to live in a series of ice ages may have been unable to adapt to the sudden changes.

The woolly mammoth was one of the victims of the Great Pleistocene Die-off.

Where Did All the Giants Go?

THE TANK THAT WALKED

6

Big, slow-moving glyptodonts depended on their armor for protection.

IT MUST HAVE BEEN an amazing sight.

Imagine standing at the edge of a shallow marshy lake in Florida about 12,000 years ago. The day is warm and muggy. Insects buzz through the tall grass, and you can see small fish flitting about in the shallow water.

A splashing sound makes you look up. Something that looks like a stone igloo is trundling toward you along the water's edge. Short legs as thick and sturdy as pillars shuffle across the muddy shore, and toes covered by hooflike sheaths spread as the animal's weight settles on them. It comes closer and you can see its long tail, encased in rings of armor, swinging from side to side as it walks.

And it's big—as big as a small car!

The animal stops, wraps its fleshy mouth around a marsh plant, tears off some leaves, and chews, gazing around. It spots you and stares. And then it ignores you. You're not a threat.

Not much could threaten a glyptodont.

Tank Division in the Mammal army

GLYPTODONTS (GLIP-TOH-DONTS) were ancient relatives of living armadillos. Armadillos have armor too, but not on the glyptodont scale!

These odd animals were protected by an igloo-shaped structure called a carapace. In a big animal, such as the one in Florida, the carapace was made up of more than a thousand bony plates, or scutes, some of them as thick as two boards.

Besides the huge carapace, the glyptodont also had a helmet, like a skullcap made of scutes. Its tail, which stuck out behind the carapace, was enclosed by rings of bone. In some South American species, the tail ended in a spiked bony knob like a medieval knight's mace. A few glyptodont skulls found in South America have holes that might have been made by the knobs, and some scientists think that glyptodonts could have used their tails in battle over territory or mates.

A drawing of a glyptodont skeleton shows how much armor the animal toted around.

The carapace isn't a kind of house that the animal lives in, like a snail shell. Instead, the carapace and the rest of the armor evolved from bony plates embedded in the hide of a glyptodont ancestor. In glyptodonts, the plates joined together to create the mammal equivalent of an armored tank.

And it was heavy armor! The carapace of a large glyptodont weighed about as much as five grown men. That's 20 percent of the animal's entire body weight. In comparison, the tusks of an elephant are only about 3 percent of its weight.

To carry all that weight, glyptodonts developed specialized load-bearing skeletons. Most of the weight was supported by the animal's hind legs and pelvis (hip bones). In addition, a short section of spine was fused and joined with the pelvis as part of the load-bearing structure.

The glyptodont's hind leg bones were enormous, extremely wide for their length. The kneecaps could lock the leg straight when the animal was resting. Although its front legs weren't as large as the back legs and supported less weight, they were still heavily built.

61

The Tank that Walked

FUN Facts

Glyptodont means carved or grooved tooth. The name comes from the glyptodont's teeth, which are wide and molar-like, and have grooves that look as if they were carved into the tooth.

Armor must have come in handy for glyptodonts. Among the predators ranging through North and South America in the Pleistocene were saber-tooth cats, scimitar cats, and huge meat-eating birds with beaks as big as suitcases!

A baby nine-banded armadillo hides beneath a plant.

Armadillos are good swimmers, but sometimes they choose to walk across streams. They let themselves sink to the bottom of the stream and walk across, holding their breath for up to six minutes.

The armadillo is the only species other than humans that can catch leprosy (also called Hansen's disease), a bacterial disease that causes skin and nerve damage.

The nine-banded armadillo almost always has quadruplets—four identical babies, all produced from a single egg.

Some armadillos have strange and wonderful names—such as the great long-nosed armadillo, the northern naked-tailed armadillo, and the screaming hairy armadillo.

Life as a tank

TANKS ARE HARD TO DESTROY—but they're also hard to maneuver. Glyptodonts had the same limitations.

Glyptodonts would have moved slowly and awkwardly, shifting their weight from one thick leg to another. Because their legs were short and their bodies low to the ground, they would have had trouble balancing on rough ground or slopes. Some scientists suspect that the animals swung their muscular tails back and forth as they walked to help them balance—like a tightrope walker carrying a pole.

Glyptodonts probably spent their lives roaming slowly through fields and along the edges of wetlands, tearing up vegetation and grinding it with their great, grooved teeth. Their fossils are common in the vast prairies of southern Argentina, in an area called Patagonia. In the southern United States, the northernmost edge of their range, they lived along the edges of rivers and shallow lakes.

How do we know that? After all, you can't ask a glyptodont.

One way to figure out where extinct animals lived is to look at where their bones are buried and what's buried with them. That's why paleontologists excavate fossils very carefully and keep detailed records of everything around the fossils, including rock layers and the remains of other animals and plants.

In the southern United States, most glyptodont fossils have been found in rock created from the sediment of streams and wetlands, even in places where streams no longer flow.

Another clue is capybara fossils. In the southern states, glyptodont and capybara fossils are commonly found together.

Capybaras still exist in South America. They're big rodents—a bit like very large, long-legged guinea pigs—and they inhabit semi-tropical wetlands. The fact that they lived together with glyptodonts suggests that the two species may have used the wetland environment in the same way.

63

The capybara is the largest rodent in the modern world. Its fossil bones have been found near those of glyptodonts in many places.

TANKS OF ALL SHAPES
AND SIZES

LIKE CAPYBARAS, GLYPTODONTS evolved in South America at a time when it was separated from North America by a deep ocean. After the Panamanian land bridge formed about 3 million years ago, a few glyptodont species moved north, along with many other South American animals.

The glyptodonts disappeared at the end of the last ice age during the Great Pleistocene Die-off. Their much smaller relatives, the armadillos, survived. Today armadillos live in South America, Central America, and southern areas of North America.

Armadillos are just as strange as their big extinct cousins. They are the only surviving mammals with bony skin armor, but their armor isn't the heavy, rigid stuff the glyptodonts developed. Instead, they have bands of armor separated by bands of tough skin that act like hinges, allowing the animals to bend.

The armor isn't nearly as thick and strong as a glyptodont's, so it doesn't provide as much protection. However, it's also not as restrictive as the glyptodont's carapace, so armadillos don't need as much protection. Unlike glyptodonts, they can run and hide!

GiaNts aND PiNK FairieS

MOST OF TODAY'S 20 SPECIES of armadillo live in Central and South America. They are a strange and wonderful collection of beasts.

The largest is the giant armadillo, about the size of a bulldog. Hinged armor plates cover its back and neck. Smaller plates embedded in its skin cover most of the rest of its body.

Using the huge claws on its front feet, the giant armadillo tears up the ground in search of prey—mainly ants and termites, but occasionally lizards and small snakes. It can scoop up hundreds of termites with one sweep of its long, sticky tongue. The giant armadillo has about a hundred teeth in its narrow muzzle—but they're small and peglike, and not much use.

In Brazil, a six-banded armadillo prepares to scoop up a berry with its tongue.

The Tank that Walked

The smallest of all living armadillos is the pink fairy armadillo. It's a delicate little creature about the size of a large mouse, which lives in central Argentina. And it really is pink. A pale pink armored cloak covers the top of its body from just behind its nose to its tail. The rest of the body, including part of the body under the armor, is covered with long, fine white hair. The pink fairy digs its burrow near an anthill, so that breakfast, lunch, and dinner are right on its doorstep!

The prize for best engineering goes to the southern three-banded armadillo. About the size of a small rabbit, it has a pointy nose and triangular tail. Around its middle, three bands of tough, flexible skin make a joint between two bowl-shaped sections of body armor. A triangular slab of armor covers its head, and armor plating protects its short tail.

The three-banded armadillo doesn't look like a marvel of engineering—until something threatens it. Then it folds the two bowl-shaped halves of its body armor into a ball, and slots the armored triangles of head and tail together to plug the remaining gap. There it waits, looking like a knobby coconut, until the threat has gone away.

A three-banded armadillo rolls into a protective ball.

ARMADILLO FAMILY TIES

GLYPTODONTS AND ARMADILLOS belong to an order called Xenarthra and they probably evolved from a small insect-eater that lived in the time of the dinosaurs.

By the time they show up in the fossil record, in the Miocene epoch, the various xenarthran groups—sloths, anteaters, glyptodonts, and armadillos—had already started to go their separate ways.

Sloths grew bigger and hairier and became plant-eaters instead of insect-eaters.

Anteaters stuck with eating insects and developed specialized mouths and tongues for the job.

The armored xenarthrans—glyptodonts and armadillos—stayed closest in appearance to their small armadillo-like ancestors. They split into three main groups: glyptodonts, giant armadillos, and armadillos. Only the armadillos survive today.

Each of those groups started with the same basic body plan and headed off in a slightly different direction. Giant armadillos grew almost as big as glyptodonts, but with a flexible armor design like modern armadillos. Glyptodonts developed the most extreme form of body armor—a heavy, rigid carapace that got heavier as the species got larger.

The surviving armadillos stayed fairly small, more flexible than glyptodonts, and surprisingly quick. They're good at running and hiding, and at burrowing with their big xenarthran claws. Many species feed at night when fewer predators are around.

Armadillo armor isn't nearly as strong as glyptodont armor, but it doesn't need to be. It protects the animal in a different way.

Strange as it seems, the anteater is a relative of both the armadillo and the sloth.

A coyote could bite through the bony armor of most armadillos, but first it would have to get its mouth around the animal. That's not as easy as it sounds.

Caught in the open, most armadillos frantically dig a shallow hole in the ground and then hunker down in it, huddling under their body armor and gripping the earth with their claws. The armor plates form a smooth surface that the coyote can't get a grip on, making it very hard to pry an armadillo out of its refuge. Eventually, if the armadillo is lucky, the coyote gives up and goes away.

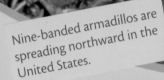

Nine-banded armadillos are spreading northward in the United States.

ARMADILLO explorers

THE NINE-BANDED ARMADILLO is the most adventurous of the tribe. It gets its name from nine bands of bone and flexible skin that separate the front and back halves of its body armor.

The nine-banded armadillo is the only living armadillo to reach North America, and it's still pushing northward. Armadillos crossed from Mexico into southern Texas around 1850. Since then, nine-banded armadillos have expanded their range northward—with a little accidental help from humans. The Florida population, for example, began with escapees from a zoo and a traveling circus!

So far, armadillos have reached South Carolina, Alabama, Mississippi, Oklahoma, southern Kansas, Arkansas, western Tennessee, southern Missouri, and southern Illinois. A few have even been spotted as far north as Nebraska.

Temperature is one of the few things that will stop a nine-banded armadillo. These mammals are not very good at regulating their own temperatures. They don't have much fat for insulation, so they need a warm climate. However, the changing global climate could allow them to move farther north.

So far, mountains have kept armadillos from expanding west to the Pacific Ocean. The mountain ranges are too high and cold for the animals to cross. However, much of the Pacific coast is warm enough for armadillos, and an accidental release of captive animals—as happened in Florida—could be all the help they need.

A six-banded armadillo glares suspiciously at the camera.

The Tank that Walked

WHICH WAY IS UP?

Fossils are like pieces from a jigsaw puzzle. Unfortunately, we only have a few pieces, and they come from a lot of different puzzles. Getting the picture right is ... well, it's tricky.

For example, take the Iguanodon.

Usually, only a few bits of an animal's skeleton survive, jumbled together and often mixed with bones from other animals. That's how Iguanodon, an early Cretaceous dinosaur, got a horn.

▶ The first attempt to reconstruct Iguanodon showed it with a curved horn on its nose.

▶ Years later, after more complete skeletons were found, scientists realized that the horn wasn't a horn at all, and it didn't fit on Iguanodon's nose. It was a spike that belonged on the dinosaur's front foot, roughly where a thumb would be.

Consider also the problem of the wonderfully named *Hallucigenia*, a little wormlike creature from the Precambrian seas, well over 500 million years ago.

Animals can take a beating on the way to becoming fossils. Sometimes they're squashed as thin as a piece of paper, with legs, wings, antennae, and tentacles sticking out every which way.

70

Fossils are often found in a jumbled heap, like these dinosaur bones. Sometimes it's hard to put them back together correctly.

How can you tell what it is, or even which way is up?

▶ *Hallucigenia* had a double set of long spines on one side of its body and a row of shorter tentacles on the other.

▶ Some scientists thought the spikes were legs, and the tentacles, some kind of feeding mechanism. Others thought the spikes protected the animal's back, and the tentacles were legs.

▶ But there seemed to be only one row of tentacles. How could the creature walk?

▶ Then a paleontologist carefully dissected a paper-thin fossil of *Hallucigenia* and found the marks of a second row of tentacles—or legs—under the first row. That turned *Hallucigenia* upside down. Or right side up. For now, at least.

71

Which Way Is Up?

The giant beaver *Castoroides* lived in North American wetlands thousands of years ago.

SUPER RODENT 7

LONG AGO, THE OJIBWAY HERO Nanabush quarreled with the giant beaver, Waub-Ameek. Nanabush and his grandmother, Nokomis, chased Waub-Ameek from lake to lake and marsh to marsh, but couldn't catch him.

Finally they found his great dam of logs and stones built across the outlet of Lake Superior. Behind the dam, the lake was rising higher and higher. Nanabush decided to go around the lake looking for the beaver, while Nokomis waited at the dam in case Waub-Ameek returned.

The giant beaver did return, and Nokomis grabbed his tail. Waub-Ameek struggled and struggled. Finally, he twisted around and began to burrow into his own dam. He dug away dirt and stones and branches until the dam broke and the mighty waters of the lake rushed through the gap. Nokomis stepped back to safety and, in that moment, Waub-Ameek yanked his tail free and escaped down the river.

72

Super Crocs & Monster Wings

Eventually, Nanabush and Waub-Ameek made peace, but the stones and debris from Waub-Ameek's great dam still lie in the narrow river between Lake Superior and Lake Huron. Today they are called the Thirty Thousand Islands.

Giant beavers show up in the traditional stories of a lot of North American aboriginal peoples—and they crop up in science too. The giant beaver of science is called *Castoroides ohioensis* (kas-tor-OY-deez oh-hy-oh-EN-siss).

THe MONSTer iN THe MarSH

IMAGINE A BEAVER AS BIG as a black bear. That was *Castoroides ohioensis*. Sitting up on its hind legs, it would have been at least as tall as a man. *Castoroides* was the largest rodent in ice age North America and probably the largest beaver that ever lived.

The giant beaver evolved in North America about 3 million years ago and survived until the end of the last glaciation, about 10,000 years ago. That means it was still alive when humans spread throughout North America—perhaps when people first told stories of a creature like Waub-Ameek.

Fossil teeth and bones of *Castoroides* have been found as far south as Florida and as far north as Old Crow in Canada, above the Arctic Circle. The fossils

By gnawing with their strong front teeth, beavers can topple large trees in a few hours.

Super Rodent

include three nearly complete skeletons, so we have a good idea of the beaver's size and appearance.

Judging by the bones, *Castoroides* looked much like a very large modern beaver, although the shape and size of the tail vertebrae suggest its tail was narrower, for its size, than the tails of modern beavers.

The biggest difference lies in the teeth. A modern beaver has short, smooth-surfaced cutting teeth. The giant beaver had gigantic, curved cutting teeth, as long as a railway spike and at least as thick, with ridges on the outer surfaces.

What did *Castoroides* use its huge teeth for? Scientists don't agree on the answer.

The beavers we know today live in and near water and use their smooth cutting teeth to gnaw on trees. Ancient beavers were a much more diverse group.

THE DEVIL'S CORKSCREWS

PALAEOCASTOR (PAY-LEE-OH-CASS-TOR) is an example of how different ancient beavers could be.

In the badlands of Nebraska, thick spiral tubes reach down into the ground as deep as the basement of a house. Enclosed in a fibrous material and filled with sand, they can sometimes be seen eroding out of the sides of hills.

More than a century ago, local ranchers named the tubes "devil's corkscrews." Later, a passing geologist called them *daimonelix* (day-moh-NEE-lix)—which is simply Latin for "devil's corkscrew."

The geologist thought the formations were the remains of giant freshwater sponges or huge fossil plants. But one of them contained the bones of a small rodent—and that was the clue paleontologists needed. The giant corkscrews are actually the remains of burrows. The creature that dug them 22 million years ago was *Palaeocastor*, a dry-land beaver about the size of a woodchuck.

A bit of luck preserved important information about how *Palaeocastor* dug. Silica from volcanic material in the soil seeped into some of the burrow walls and turned them hard. *Palaeocastor*'s excavation marks can still be seen—and the marks were made by teeth!

This beaver used its teeth to dig, not its claws like most burrowing animals. Fossil remains of *Palaeocastor* show that it had very long front teeth that kept growing throughout its life, a handy characteristic for an animal that grinds its teeth against sand.

The excavation marks even show why *Palaeocastor* burrows are spiral-shaped. The tooth marks are set at an angle. The beaver scraped its way around and around the walls of its burrow, going deeper with each circuit, just like a screw going into wood. Once the burrow was deep enough, the little animal dug sideways to create cozy spaces for nesting and eating.

In 1893, American paleontologist Frederick C. Kenyon posed beside a fossilized burrow of the extinct beaver, *Palaeocastor.*

FOLLOWING the LAKES

CASTOROIDES WAS MUCH TOO LARGE to build the kind of burrow that *Palaeocastor* lived in, and all the evidence indicates that it was semi-aquatic like modern beavers.

Fossils of giant beavers are often found in deposits left by marshy lakes, the same kind of place today's beavers prefer. In some areas, *Castoroides* and the modern North American beaver, *Castor canadensis (CAS-tor cah-nah-DEN-siss),* lived side by side.

But did *Castoroides* build dams, like the mighty Waub-Ameek? So far, there's no proof one way or the other. Plenty of ancient beaver-chewed wood has been found, but none that can be positively linked to giant beavers.

75

Swimming back home, this beaver easily pushes a freshly cut branch through the water.

Modern beavers still live in the same kind of habitat. So why are there no longer any giant beavers?

Castoroides is one of the large mammals that died out at the end of the last glaciation. It's possible that humans hunted the beaver, but so far no one has found a kill site or other evidence.

Another possibility is that giant beavers were affected by the changing climate. They depended on marshy lakes for food. An animal as big as *Castoroides* needed plenty of food, so if the marshy lakes started to dry up, *Castoroides* could have been in trouble.

Moving to a new lake might not have been an option. The giant beaver's hind legs were too short and it was too heavy to walk any great distance. Shifting ice could have blocked the way. *Castoroides* might simply have run out of good swamps.

Either hunting or habitat loss could explain the disappearance of the giant beaver, or the explanation might still lie buried with the fossil remains of an undiscovered giant.

FUN Facts

Although the giant beaver was much larger than modern beavers, its brain was about the same size.

For almost 300 years, beginning in the 16th century, Europeans had a passion for felt hats made from beaver fur. Trapping to supply the fur almost drove the beaver to extinction before the fashion switched to silk hats around 1840.

Today there are between 6 and 12 million beavers in North America, from the arctic treeline to northern Mexico.

Beavers are stilled trapped for human use. Their scent glands produce a substance called castoreum. Today it's used in some perfumes. In the past, it was used as a medicine for headaches and fevers.

Water still dripping from its well-groomed fur, a beaver sticks its head up to look around.

On the second toe of each hind foot, beavers have specialized double claws, like tiny pliers, which they use to comb dirt out of their fur and coat it with oil from special glands. This careful grooming keeps their fur warm and waterproof.

Fossils of an extinct beaver called *Dipoides* (dih-POY-deez), along with more than a hundred specimens of beaver-cut wood, have been found on Canada's Ellesmere Island, not far from the north pole. No tree has grown there in millions of years.

BEAVER FAMILY TIES

THE BEAVERS ORIGINATED as a separate family of rodents in the late Eocene epoch, perhaps 35 million years ago. Over all that time, there have been about 30 branches of the beaver family, and scientists are still trying to figure out how they are related.

According to one theory, the beaver family split into dry-land, burrowing groups, and swimming groups quite early in its development.

The burrowing animals, which are all extinct, lived in grasslands and open woodlands in North America. *Palaeocastor*, creator of the devil's corkscrew burrows, is a member of this group.

The swimming beavers lived near streams and lakes and became semi-aquatic, spending part of their lives in water. Swimming beavers are "holoarctic." That means they are found all around the northern part of the northern hemisphere—in North America, Europe, and Asia.

Both the giant beaver *Castoroides* and modern beavers belong to the swimming group.

Not all swimming beavers used trees as building materials, the way modern beavers do. So far, we know that *Castor*, the modern beaver, and some members of an extinct genus called *Dipoides* developed this ability. *Castoroides* might also be part of this group, but we don't have enough evidence yet to be sure.

The skull of the extinct giant beaver, *Castoroides*, looms over the much smaller skull of a modern beaver.

We do know, however, that modern North American beavers are not descendants of *Castoroides*. Both of them, along with other species of swimming beavers, lived side by side in North American wetlands for as much as several million years before the giant beaver died out just 10,000 years ago.

A beaver hauls a large branch that will become part of its lodge or dam.

laKiNG tHe WORLD FIt

THE SUCCESS OF MODERN BEAVERS is easier to explain. Beavers, like humans, are experts at making the environment suit their needs. If your lake starts drying up, just build a dam!

Two closely related species of beaver survive today: the Eurasian beaver (*Castor fiber*) and the North American beaver (*Castor canadensis*). Eurasian beavers simply dig burrows in the riverbank, but North American beavers build their own lodges. And both of them build dams.

Beavers don't build dams everywhere—only where they're needed. In northern climates, the water around a lodge has to be deep enough that it doesn't freeze in winter and block the underwater entrance. If the water isn't deep enough, the beaver builds a dam to make it deeper.

First, the beaver lays a row of sticks and rocks in the streambed, pushing some of the sticks into the mud. If it can't find rocks, it will use whatever is available. One enterprising prehistoric beaver in the Yukon used the bone of a mammoth in its dam.

79

Super Rodent

Inside a cozy lodge, this beaver and its kits can stay snug and warm all winter.

The beaver adds more layers until the dam is strong enough to hold back the stream and keep the water level high. Some beavers have built dams as high as a street lamp.

If you've ever seen a big pile of sticks in the middle of a pond or attached to the bank of a lake or slow river, you've probably seen a beaver lodge. The beaver collects branches, twigs, and stones, and glues them together with mud until a solid cone rises out of the water. Then it digs an underwater entrance into the lodge and hollows out a comfy, well-insulated home with a dry nesting area, a feeding chamber, and a vent to keep the air fresh.

On the bottom of the pond, the beaver assembles its food pile. During the summer, both species of beaver eat many kinds of plants, but their main winter food is twigs from leafy trees such as poplar and aspen. As soon as the weather starts turning cold, beavers collect twigs, branches, and even small trees. They haul their loot into the pond and anchor it to the bottom, ready for snacking through the winter.

Gathering the winter food supply is a big job. The twigs and branches required to get a beaver family through the winter would fill a couple of pickup trucks.

GOOD DAMS
AND GOOD NEIGHBORS

THE BEAVER'S DAM-BUILDING HABIT makes it a good neighbor to some and a bad neighbor to others.

Beaver ponds can reduce seasonal flooding by trapping and slowing spring meltwater in streams. They create habitat for plants, amphibians, fish, birds, and hundreds of different kinds of invertebrates. Moose browse on the vegetation in beaver ponds, ducks nest among the reeds, and herons stalk through the shallows watching for fish.

The beaver's urge to build dams can also flood forests and farmland, wash away roads, block culverts, and divert streams.

In some parts of the world, North American beavers have become dam-building disasters.

Sixty years ago, a few pairs of North American beavers were introduced to the island of Tierra del Fuego, at the southern tip of South America, in order to start a fur industry. The beavers multiplied faster than they were trapped and now the dams and ponds of 100,000 beavers are destroying the native landscape.

Good dams don't always make good neighbors.

The master builder of the animal world at work: a beaver pushes a new branch into its dam.

Super Rodent

Although they seem fragile, dragonflies have survived for more than 300 million years.

A POSTSCRIPT IS SOMETHING that comes after a book or letter. So—what comes after this book? What will the future bring for the animals we've spent time with here?

The world has changed dramatically over the past few hundreds of millions of years. Continents have collided and separated. Towering mountain ranges have risen and worn away. Massive ice sheets have crushed the land, sucked up the sea, then retreated, leaving new landscapes behind. Even the air itself has altered over time.

And the world continues to change. The climate is warming. Sea levels are rising. Deserts are expanding in some parts of the world, while new wetlands appear in other regions. Humans are part of the change. We log forests, build dams, plant crops, and expand our cities. Those activities have an impact on the world around us.

So far, the animal families in this book have all survived.

Some family members have disappeared, but their relatives carry on, adapting to change and changing themselves. Dragonflies have flourished through more than 300 million years and, though the giant dragonflies are gone, their smaller relatives flit over ponds and marshes around the world. The giant ground sloths died out, but their little cousins retreated to the treetops to live. *Sarcosuchus* vanished and its river home turned to desert, but crocodilians, which have been on the planet since the time of the dinosaurs, still thrive today. They live on almost every continent—in rivers, lakes, tidal estuaries, coastal lagoons, and mangrove swamps.

82

Which of our animal families will survive the changes to come?

Camels almost disappeared, but their value to humans as domestic animals gives them an advantage today. The sloth family found safety in the trees, but their home forests in Central and South America are shrinking. If those forested areas diminish more, will they need to find another safe haven? In contrast, the warming climate is creating new habitat suitable for the glyptodont's relatives, armadillos, and they are moving into it. And beavers have the skills to make their own habitat, whatever the weather does.

What we don't know and can't predict is: what might our animal families become, tens or hundreds of thousands of years from now?

The world can change very quickly for living things, including humans. Here, lava from an active volcano flows across a road, leaving a huge wall of hot rock where people walked and drove just hours earlier.

Further Reading

DRAGONFLIES

Nikula, Blair, and Jackie Sones, with Donald and Lillian Stokes. *Stokes Beginner's Guide to Dragonflies*. Boston: Little, Brown & Co., 2002.

Ode News. www.odenews.org. Internet newsletter and website about dragonflies.

Look in a library or bookstore for a field guide to dragonflies in your area. The guide will have information about how the dragonflies live, where they live, and how to tell them apart.

CROCODILIANS

Crocodilians: Natural History & Conservation. www.crocodilian.com. Hosted by the Crocodile Specialist Group, an international organization devoted to the study and conservation of crocodiles and their relatives.

Dudley, Karen. *The Untamed World: Alligators and Crocodiles*. Calgary, AB: Weigl Educational Publishers, 1998.

Sloan, Christopher. *SuperCroc and the Origin of Crocodiles*. Washington, DC: National Geographic, 2002.

CAMELS

Brian, Janeen. *Hoosh! Camels in Australia*. Sydney, Australia: ABC Books for the Australian Broadcasting Corporation, 2005.

Harington, C.R. *Ice Age Yukon and Alaskan Camels*. Beringian Research Notes, No. 10. Whitehorse, YT: Yukon Department of Tourism & Culture, 1997. Available online at www.beringia.com/02/02maina10.html.

Wexo, John Bonnett. *Camels (Zoobooks)*. Poway, California: Wildlife Education, 1999.

SLOTHS

Harington, C.R. *Jefferson's Ground Sloth*. Beringian Research Notes, No. 1. Whitehorse, YT: Yukon Department of Tourism & Culture, 1993. Available online at www.beringia.com/02/02maina1.html.

Squire, Ann O. *Anteaters, Sloths, and Armadillos*. New York: Franklin Watts, 1999.

Stewart, Melissa. *Sloths (Nature Watch)*. Minneapolis: Lerner Publications, 2005.

GLYPTODONTS AND ARMADILLOS

Potts, Steve. *The Armadillo (Wildlife of North America)*. Mankato, MN: Capstone Press, 1998.

Squire, Ann O. *Anteaters, Sloths, and Armadillos*. New York: Franklin Watts, 1999.

Stuart, Dee. *The Astonishing Armadillo (Nature Watch)*. Minneapolis: Lerner Publications, 1993.

BEAVERS

Harington, C.R. *Giant Beaver*. Beringian Research Notes, No. 6. Whitehorse, YT: Yukon Department of Tourism & Culture, 1996. Available online at www.beringia.com/02/02maina6.html.

Kitchener, Andrew. *Beavers*. British Natural History Series. Stowmarket, Suffolk: Whittet Books, 2001.

Rue, Dr. Leonard Lee, III. *Beavers*. World Wildlife Library. Stillwater, MN: Voyageur Press, 2002.

Swanson, Diane. *Welcome to the World of Beavers*. Vancouver: Whitecap Books, 1999.

GENERAL

Bonner, Hannah. *When Bugs Were Big, Plants Were Strange, and Tetrapods Stalked the Earth*. Washington, DC: National Geographic, 2004.

Camper, Cathy. *Bugs Before Time: Prehistoric Insects and Their Relatives*. New York: Simon & Schuster Books for Young Readers, 2002.

Lange, Ian M. *Ice Age Mammals of North America: A Guide to the Big, the Hairy, and the Bizarre*. Missoula, MT: Mountain Press Publishing, 2002.

Savage, R.J.G., and M.R. Long. *Mammal Evolution: An Illustrated Guide*. New York: Facts On File Publications, 1986.

Attenborough, David. *The Life of Mammals.* Princeton, NJ: Princeton University Press, 2002.

Cannings, Robert A. *Introducing the Dragonflies of British Columbia and the Yukon.* Victoria, BC: Royal British Columbia Museum, 2002.

Cohen, Daniel. *The Age of Giant Mammals.* New York: Dodd, Mead & Co., 1969.

Fortey, Richard. *Fossils: The Key to the Past.* 3rd ed. Washington, DC: Smithsonian Institution Press, 2002.

Fountain, Henry. "When Giants had Wings and 6 Legs." *New York Times.* February 3, 2004.

Gillette, David D., and Clayton E. Ray. *Glyptodonts of North America.* Smithsonian Contributions to Paleobiology Number 40. Washington, DC: Smithsonian Institution Press, 1981.

Harington, C.R. *Giant Beaver.* Beringian Research Notes, No. 6. Whitehorse, YT: Yukon Department of Tourism & Culture, 1996.

Harington, C.R. *Ice Age Yukon and Alaskan Camels.* Beringian Research Notes, No. 10. Whitehorse, YT: Yukon Department of Tourism & Culture, 1997.

Harington, C.R. *Jefferson's Ground Sloth.* Beringian Research Notes, No. 1. Whitehorse, YT: Yukon Department of Tourism & Culture, 1993.

Kitchener, Andrew. *Beavers.* British Natural History Series. Stowmarket, Suffolk: Whittet Books, 2001.

Kurten, Bjorn, and Elaine Anderson. *Pleistocene Mammals of North America.* New York: Columbia University Press, 1980.

Lange, Ian M. *Ice Age Mammals of North America: A Guide to the Big, the Hairy, and the Bizarre.* Missoula, MT: Mountain Press, 2002.

Martin, Larry D. "The Devil's Corkscrew." *Natural History.* April 1994: 59.

Martin, Paul S. *Twilight of the Mammoths: Ice Age Extinctions and the Rewilding of America.* Berkeley, CA: University of California Press, 2005.

Menon, Shanti. "Insects of the Oxygeniferous." *Discover Magazine.* September 1, 1995.

Poinar, Hendrik N.; Michael Hofreiter; W. Geoffrey Spaulding; Paul S. Martin; B. Artur Staniewicz; Helen Bland; Richard P. Evershed; Goran Possnert; and Svante Paabo. "Molecular Coproscopy: Dung and Diet of the Extinct Ground Sloth *Nothrotheriops shastensis.*" *Science.* July 17, 1998: 402ff.

Ross, Jen. "A Canadian Beaver in Chile." *Walrus Magazine.* May 2006.

Salisbury, Steve. "Dawn of a Crocodilian Dynasty." *Australian Geographic.* July–September 2006: 52–53.

Savage, R.J.G., and M.R. Long. *Mammal Evolution: An Illustrated Guide.* New York: Facts On File, 1986.

Schubert, Brian W., Jim I. Mead, and Russell Wm. Graham, eds. *Ice Age Faunas of North America.* Denver Museum of Nature and Science V Series. Bloomington, IN: Indiana University Press, 2003.

Sereno, Paul C.; Hans C.E. Larsson; Christian A. Sidor; and Boubé Gado. "The Giant Crocodyliform *Sarcosuchus* from the Cretaceous of Africa." *Science.* November 16, 2001: 1516.

Sloan, Christopher. *SuperCroc and the Origin of Crocodiles.* Washington, DC: National Geographic, 2002.

Soares, Daphne. "An Ancient Sensory Organ in Crocodilians." *Nature.* May 16, 2002: 241–42.

Steadman, David W.; Paul S. Martin; Ross D.E. MacPhee; A.J.T. Jull; H. Gregory McDonald; Charles A. Woods; Manuel Iturralde-Vinent; and Gregory W.L. Hodgins. "Asynchronous Extinction of Late Quaternary Sloths on Continents and Islands." *Proceedings of the National Academy of Sciences.* August 16, 2005: 11763–68.

Turner, Alan. *Prehistoric Mammals.* Washington, DC: National Geographic, 2004.

Ward, Peter D. *Out of Thin Air: Dinosaurs, Birds, and Earth's Ancient Atmosphere.* Washington, DC: Joseph Henry Press, 2006.

Yagil, Reuven. "From Its Blood to Its Hump, the Camel Adapts to the Desert." *Natural History.* August 1993: 30.

INDEX

A

Africa, 10–11, 24, 35, 40, 45
Antarctic, 19
Antarctica, 10–11
anteaters, 55, 67
archosaurs, 33
Arctic, 19, 46, 49, 53, 73, 77, 78
Argentina, 52, 63, 66
armadillos, 55, 61, 62, 64–69, 83
armor, 26, 30–31, 52, 60, 61, 62, 64–65, 66, 67, 68
Asia, 10–11, 13, 39, 40, 41, 43, 78, 79
atmosphere, 16–17, 21, 47. *See also* oxygen
Australia, 10–11, 13, 30, 33, 44–45

B

beavers, 72–81, 83
dam-building, 75, 79–81
Dipoides, 77, 78
Eurasian beaver (*Castor fiber*), 79
fossils, 73, 74–75, 76
fur, 77, 81

beavers (cont.)
giant beaver (*Castoroides ohioensis*), 72, 73–74, 75–76, 77, 78, 79
lodge, 79–80
North American beaver (*Castor canadensis*), 75, 78, 79–81
Palaeocastor, 74–75, 78
teeth, 74, 75
Waub-Ameek, 72–73
birds, 6, 7, 33, 62
Brazil, 17, 50, 51, 65

C

camels. *See* camelids
camelids, 36–45, 58, 83
Aepycamelus, 36, 37
alpaca, 39, 43
Bactrian camel, 38, 41, 43
domestic, 39, 41, 45, 83
dromedary (Arabian camel), 38, 41, 43, 45
feet, 42
fossils, 37, 42, 43
giraffe-camels, 37, 43
guanaco, 39, 43
hump, 38, 39, 41, 43, 44, 45

camelids (cont.)
llama, 39, 40, 41, 43
Poebrotherium, 42, 43
Protolabis, 43
Protylopus, 36–37, 43
spitting, 38
stomach, 41
teeth, 38
Titanotylopus, 37
vicuña, 38, 39, 43
walk, 42
Canada, 11, 35, 73, 77
capybara, 63, 64
Carboniferous period, 8, 13, 16, 17, 19, 21
Central America, 39, 48, 56, 64
continents, 10–11, 82
coprolites, 52
Cretaceous period, 8, 23, 47, 70
Crocodiles. *See* crocodilians
crocodilians, 24–33, 34, 43, 82
alligator, 25, 27, 28, 31–32
bite, 26–27, 28, 34
bulla, 27
crocodile, 25, 26, 28, 29, 30, 33, 34, 43
Deinosuchus, 29

89

Acknowledgments

MY THANKS TO Dr. Grant Zazula, Yukon paleontologist, for his expertise on mammals, and to the folks at the Heritage Resources Unit of the Yukon Department of Tourism and Culture for letting me hang out in their library.

Thank you to Dr. Adam Britton of Big Gecko Crocodilian Research and Consulting in Darwin, Australia, for sharing his knowledge of crocodiles and all their relatives.

And thanks also to Dr. Roy J. Beckemeyer, museum associate with the Division of Entomology at the University of Kansas Natural History Museum, and devoted dragonfly scholar.

Any errors are mine, not theirs.

91

PHOtO CreDits

cover (*Sarcosuchus imperator*), 24: © John Sibbick; cover (Nile crocodile), 28: © EcoPrint/shutterstock.com; 2 (frontispiece), 25: © istockphoto.com/ susan flashman; 6: © John Kirinic/shutterstock.com; 7, 13: © Cameron Eckert; 9: © Johan Swanepoel/shutterstock.com; 11: © Ron Blakey, Northern Arizona Univ. Geology; 12: © Willem Pretorius; 14, 17: © Dr. Günter Bechly, Staatliches Museum für Naturkunde Stuttgart, Germany; 15: © RSBS/ANU/ Geoffrey Hunter; 18, 19, 82: © Elizabeth Moon; 20: © Ismael Montero Verdu/ shutterstock.com; 23: © Jozef Sedmak/shutterstock.com; 27: © Cynthia Burkhardt/shutterstock.com; 29: © Andre Maritz/shutterstock.com; 31: © Dmitry Tsiplakov/shutterstock.com; 32, 33: © emin kuliyev/shutterstock. com; 35: image*after; 36, 60: Heinrich Harder illustrations, courtesy of search4dinosaurs.com; 38: © Nir Levy/shutterstock.com; 39: © Grigory Kubatyan/shutterstock.com; 40: © istockphoto.com/Kornelis Bakker; 42: © istockphoto.com/Burghard Drews; 43: © Harald Høiland Tjøstheim/ shutterstock.com; 44, 71: © Styve Reineck/shutterstock.com; 45: © istockphoto.com/Alexander Hafemann; 46, 50, 78: © Claire Eamer; 47: © michael ledray/shutterstock.com; 48, 53, 59, 72: © Carl Buell; 51, 69: © Alvaro Pantoja/shutterstock.com; 52: © A. Gordon Edmund; 54: © Gregory James Van Raalte/shutterstock.com; 55, 57: © Steffen Foerster Photography/ shutterstock.com; 56: © stockbyte/First Light; 61: Joseph Smit drawing, courtesy of search4dinosaurs.com; 62: © istockphoto.com/Norman Morin; 64: © istockphoto.com/Flavia Bottazzini; 65: © istockphoto.com/Greg Brzezinski; 66: © Mark Payne-Gill, Nature Picture Library; 67: © istockphoto.com/ Michael Chen; 68: photo by John and Karen Hollingsworth/U.S. Fish and Wildlife Service; 73: © Peggy Easterly/shutterstock.com; 75: courtesy of The University of Nebraska State Museum; 76: © istockphoto.com/jeffrey hochstrasser; 77: © Jason Kasumovic/shutterstock.com; 79: © 3483253554/ shutterstock.com; 80: © Photoresearchers/First Light; 81: © John Meikle; 83: © istockphoto.com/koch valérie

ABOUT THE AUTHOR

CLAIRE EAMER grew up on the prairies in Saskatchewan and now lives in the mountains of the Yukon, and she loves them both. She is a full-time writer who likes books, gadgets, traveling, and asking questions. Writing about science lets her ask as many questions as she wants—so she likes to write about science.

93

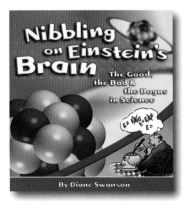

Nibbling on Einstein's Brain: The Good, the Bad and the Bogus in Science

Text by Diane Swanson
Illustrated by Warren Clark

- *Booklist*'s Top 10 Sci-Tech Books for Youth
- *VOYA*'s Non-Fiction Honor List
- Best Books of the Year List & Editor's Choice List, Science Books & Films
- White Raven Collection, International Youth Library, Munich
- Eisenhower Collection of Math and Science Books
- Los Angeles 100 Best Books List, IRA

"This fascinating and kid-friendly book gives budding scientists and others an introduction to the tools and strategies needed to evaluate and understand scientific information... The strategies learned here can easily be applied to history and social science research, making this title an intriguing choice for any school or public library." —*School Library Journal*

"... a good introduction to bad science... with a highly readable text and jaunty line illustrations, the book encourages critical thinking..." —*Booklist*

Ages 9–13 | Paperback $14.95 US / $16.95 Cdn | Hardcover $24.95

Turn It Loose: The Scientist in Absolutely Everybody

Text by Diane Swanson
Illustrations by Warren Clark

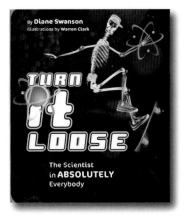

"Buy this for the sheer quantity of information and the excellent 'Brainplay' activities concluding each chapter." —*Booklist*

"This fun, lighthearted romp through history shows young people that they really do have a scientist inside them. Swanson effortlessly ties in all the major approaches of science... Solid, clear, and informative illustrations help bring the text to life." —*VOYA*

"... relentlessly enthusiastic esteem-builder..." —*Kirkus Reviews*

Ages 10–14 | Paperback $14.95 US / $16.95 Cdn | Hardcover $29.95

It's True! An Octopus Has Deadly Spit

Written and illustrated by Nicki Greenberg

• Shortlisted for the Royal Society's Aventis Prizes for Science Books 2006 Junior Prize

"One of the most fascinating kids' nature books I've read… extremely readable… Greenberg's natural wonder for these animals is infectious." —*The Toronto Star*

Fascinating facts about octopi and squid dished up with delectable humor.

Ages 8–13 | Paperback $5.95 US / $6.95 Cdn | Hardcover $19.95

It's True! There Are Bugs in Your Bed

By Heather Catchpole and Vanessa Woods
Illustrated by Craig Smith

The squirmiest book on bugs you'll ever read.

Blood-sucking vampires, deadly dust-dwellers, toilet terrors, and things that squish, squirm, and slime. Did you have any idea you were sharing your house—and maybe your bed—with monsters?

Ages 8–13 | Paperback $5.95 US / $6.95 Cdn | Hardcover $19.95

It's True! We Came From Slime

By Ken McNamara
Illustrated by Andrew Plant

"Ken McNamara's lively words may draw in science-minded kids reading on their own, and teachers may want to borrow from McNamara's creative examples." —*Booklist*

The wildest book about prehistoric life you'll ever read.

Ages 8–11 | Paperback $5.95 US / $6.95 Cdn | Hardcover $19.95